PLANT BASED

COOKING

**EASY, WHOLESOME AND DELICIOUS
RECIPES FOR GOOD HEALTH**

Publications International, Ltd.

Photograph on front cover (top left) and page 95 © Shutterstock.com.

Pictured on the front cover *(top to bottom):* Soba Miso Bowl *(page 94)* and Farro, Grape and Roasted Carrot Bowl *(page 114)*.

Pictured on the back cover *(clockwise from top left):* Cauliflower Tacos with Chipotle Crema *(page 72)*, Zoodles in Tomato Sauce *(page 141)*, Taco Salad To Go *(page 44)*, Hearty Veggie Sandwich *(page 117)* and Garden Vegetable Soup *(page 54)*.

ISBN: 978-1-64030-635-6

Manufactured in China.

8 7 6 5 4 3 2 1

CONTENTS

chapters:

ICON KEY

(NF) NUT FREE

(Q) QUICK PREP

(GF) GLUTEN FREE

(EF) EGG FREE

(V) VEGAN

(DF) DAIRY FREE

(MA) MAKE AHEAD

Berry Buckwheat Scones

Makes 8 scones

1. Preheat oven to 375°F. Line baking sheet with parchment paper.

2. Combine all-purpose flour, ¼ cup buckwheat flour, palm sugar, baking powder and salt in bowl of food processor; pulse until combined. Add butter; pulse until pea-sized pieces of butter remain. Transfer mixture to large bowl; stir in berries.

3. Whisk egg and cream in small bowl. Stir cream mixture into flour mixture until soft dough forms.

4. Transfer dough to work surface lightly dusted with buckwheat flour; gently pat into an 8-inch round about ¾ inch thick. Cut into 8 wedges.

5. Place wedges 1½ inches apart on prepared baking sheet. Sprinkle tops with turbinado sugar, if desired. Bake 20 to 25 minutes or until golden. Remove to wire rack; cool 10 minutes.

6. Serve warm with jam or lemon curd, if desired.

1¼ cups all-purpose flour

¾ cup buckwheat flour, plus additional for dusting

¼ cup palm sugar or packed brown sugar

1 tablespoon baking powder

½ teaspoon salt

½ cup (1 stick) cold butter, cubed

¾ cup fresh raspberries

¾ cup fresh blackberries

1 egg

½ cup whipping cream

1 tablespoon turbinado sugar (optional)

Jam or lemon curd (optional)

BREAKFAST AND BRUNCH

Spinach, Artichoke and Asiago Quiche

Makes 6 servings

1 **Gluten-Free Pie Crust (page 7)***

1½ **cups half-and-half**

3 **eggs**

1¼ **cups shredded Asiago cheese, divided**

¼ **teaspoon salt**

¼ **teaspoon black pepper**

¼ **teaspoon ground nutmeg**

2 **teaspoons Dijon mustard**

1 **package (10 ounces) frozen chopped spinach, thawed and squeezed dry**

1 **cup water-packed quartered artichokes, pressed dry and chopped**

*Or use your favorite regular pie crust recipe or a frozen deep-dish pie crust.

1. Prepare pie crust.

2. Preheat oven to 375°F. Lightly grease 9-inch pie plate. Roll out crust on lightly floured surface into 11-inch circle. Place in prepared plate. Flute edge as desired. Bake 20 minutes.

3. Meanwhile, whisk half-and-half and eggs in medium bowl until well blended. Stir in ¾ cup cheese, salt, pepper and nutmeg.

4. *Reduce oven temperature to 350°F.* Spread mustard over crust. Layer evenly with spinach and artichokes, pressing down lightly into crust. Pour egg mixture evenly over vegetables. Top evenly with remaining ½ cup cheese.

5. Bake 40 minutes or until knife inserted into center comes out clean. Let stand at least 10 minutes before serving. Serve warm or at room temperature.

TIP: If edges are browning too quickly in oven, cover with a strip of aluminum foil.

Gluten-Free Pie Crust

Makes 1 (9-inch pie crust)

1 cup gluten-free all-purpose flour blend,* plus additional for work surface

2 tablespoons rice flour

1½ teaspoons sugar

½ teaspoon xanthan gum

¼ teaspoon salt

6 tablespoons (¾ stick) cold butter, cubed

1 egg

2 teaspoons cider vinegar

Choose a blend that does not contain xanthan gum.

1. Combine 1 cup flour blend, rice flour, sugar, xanthan gum and salt in medium bowl; mix well. Cut in butter with pastry blender or pulse in food processor until mixture forms coarse crumbs.

2. Make a well in center of mixture. Add egg and vinegar. Stir together just until dough forms. (If dough is dry and does not hold together, add 1 tablespoon cold water at a time until dough sticks together when pressed). Shape dough into flat disc. Wrap in plastic wrap and refrigerate at least 45 minutes or until very cold. Crust can be made a day in advance.

Cranberry Buttermilk Pancakes

Makes 18 (3-inch) pancakes

1 cup all-purpose flour

1 cup whole wheat flour

2 teaspoons baking powder

1 teaspoon baking soda

½ teaspoon ground cinnamon

¼ teaspoon ground nutmeg

⅔ cup whole berry cranberry sauce

2 eggs

2 tablespoons vegetable oil, plus additional for cooking

1½ cups buttermilk

Maple syrup (optional)

1. Combine all-purpose flour, whole wheat flour, baking powder, baking soda, cinnamon and nutmeg in small bowl; mix well. Whisk cranberry sauce, eggs and 2 tablespoons oil in large bowl until well blended. Gradually stir in flour mixture until combined. Stir in buttermilk until smooth and well blended.

2. Heat large nonstick griddle or skillet over medium heat. Brush with oil. Pour ¼ cupfuls of batter 2 inches apart onto griddle. Cook 3 minutes or until lightly browned and edges begin to bubble. Turn over; cook 3 minutes or until lightly browned. Repeat with remaining batter. Serve with maple syrup, if desired.

Banana-Blueberry Oat and Quinoa Cake

Makes 12 to 16 servings

2 cups old-fashioned oats

1 cup uncooked quinoa, rinsed

1 cup packed dark brown sugar or palm sugar, divided

⅔ cup all-purpose flour

1½ teaspoons ground cinnamon

1½ teaspoons baking powder

½ teaspoon salt

3 medium ripe bananas

1 cup milk

2 eggs

½ cup applesauce

2 tablespoons butter, melted

½ teaspoon vanilla

2 cups fresh blueberries, divided

½ cup chopped pecans

1. Preheat oven to 375°F. Spray 13×9-inch baking pan with nonstick cooking spray.

2. Combine oats, quinoa, ¾ cup brown sugar, flour, cinnamon, baking powder and salt in large bowl.

3. Mash bananas in medium bowl. Stir in milk, eggs, applesauce, butter and vanilla. Add to quinoa mixture; mix well. Fold in 1 cup blueberries. Spread batter in prepared pan; sprinkle with remaining blueberries, remaining ¼ cup brown sugar and pecans.

4. Bake 40 to 45 minutes or until golden brown and set. Cool in pan 10 minutes before serving. Serve warm or at room temperature. Store leftovers in refrigerator.

Spinach Artichoke Egg Soufflés

Makes 8 servings

1 package frozen puff pastry (2 sheets), thawed according to package directions

1 teaspoon olive oil

¼ cup chopped onion

1 clove garlic, minced

¼ cup finely chopped roasted red pepper (1 pepper)

¼ cup finely chopped canned artichoke hearts (about 2 medium)

¼ cup thawed frozen spinach, squeezed dry

3 eggs, separated

½ (8-ounce) package cream cheese, softened

½ teaspoon salt

⅛ teaspoon black pepper

4 tablespoons grated Romano cheese, divided

1. Preheat oven to 400°F. Spray eight 4-inch or 1-cup ramekins or jumbo (3½-inch) muffin pan cups with nonstick cooking spray. Unfold puff pastry; cut each sheet into quarters. Gently press each pastry square into bottoms and partially up sides of prepared ramekins. (Pastry should not reach tops.) Place ramekins on baking sheet; refrigerate while preparing filling.

2. Heat oil in medium skillet over medium heat. Add onion; cook and stir 2 minutes or until softened and lightly browned. Add garlic; cook and stir 30 seconds. Add roasted pepper, artichokes and spinach; cook and stir 2 minutes or until all liquid has evaporated.

3. Whisk egg yolks, cream cheese, salt and black pepper in medium bowl until well blended. Stir in vegetable mixture and 3 tablespoons Romano cheese.

4. Beat egg whites in large bowl with electric mixer at high speed 3 minutes or until stiff peaks form. Fold into vegetable mixture until blended. Divide mixture evenly among pastry-lined ramekins; sprinkle with remaining 1 tablespoon Romano cheese. Fold points of pastry towards center.

5. Bake 25 minutes or until pastry is golden brown and filling is puffed. Cool in ramekins 2 minutes; remove to wire rack. Serve warm.

MAKE AHEAD: Prepare recipe and cool completely. Wrap them up and store them in the refrigerator. Reheat them individually in the oven or toaster oven just before serving.

BREAKFAST AND BRUNCH

Fruit-Filled Puff Pancake

Makes 4 servings

½ cup all-purpose flour

¼ teaspoon salt

2 eggs

½ cup milk

1 teaspoon vanilla

1 tablespoon butter

2 cups sliced fresh strawberries

1 teaspoon granulated sugar

2 teaspoons powdered sugar

1. Preheat oven to 400°F.

2. Combine flour and salt in large bowl. Whisk eggs in medium bowl until frothy. Whisk in milk and vanilla until blended. Add to flour mixture; whisk until blended. (Batter will be slightly lumpy.)

3. Place butter in 9-inch glass pie plate. Place in oven 1 minute or until butter is bubbly. Remove from oven; swirl pan to coat bottom and sides of pie plate. Pour excess butter into batter; mix well. Pour batter into hot pie plate; bake 20 minutes or until puffed and lightly browned.

4. Meanwhile, combine strawberries and granulated sugar in medium bowl.

5. Cut puff into 4 wedges. Spoon strawberries over wedges. Sprinkle with powdered sugar. Serve immediately.

BREAKFAST AND BRUNCH

Baked Pumpkin Oatmeal

Makes 6 servings

2 cups old-fashioned oats

2 cups milk

1 cup canned pumpkin

2 eggs

⅓ cup packed brown sugar or palm sugar

1 teaspoon vanilla

½ cup dried cranberries, plus additional for topping

1 teaspoon pumpkin pie spice

½ teaspoon salt

½ teaspoon baking powder

Maple syrup

Chopped pecans (optional)

1. Preheat oven to 350°F. Spray 8-inch square baking dish with nonstick cooking spray.

2. Spread oats on ungreased baking sheet. Bake about 10 minutes or until fragrant and lightly browned, stirring occasionally. Pour into medium bowl; let cool slightly.

3. Whisk milk, pumpkin, eggs, brown sugar and vanilla in large bowl until well blended. Add ½ cup cranberries, pumpkin pie spice, salt and baking powder to oats; mix well. Add oat mixture to pumpkin mixture; stir until well blended. Pour into prepared baking dish.

4. Bake about 45 minutes or until top is set and knife inserted into center comes out almost clean. Serve warm with maple syrup, additional cranberries and pecans, if desired. Store leftovers in the refrigerator. Reheat individual servings in the microwave.

GLUTEN-FREE: To make sure this recipe is gluten-free, select gluten-free oats that have been processed in a dedicated gluten-free facility.

Baked Pumpkin French Toast

Makes 6 servings

1 tablespoon butter, softened

1 loaf challah or egg bread (12 to 16 ounces), cut into ¾-inch-thick slices

7 eggs

1¼ cups milk

⅔ cup canned pumpkin

1 teaspoon vanilla

½ teaspoon pumpkin pie spice

⅛ teaspoon salt

3 tablespoons sugar

2 teaspoons ground cinnamon

Maple syrup

1. Generously grease 13×9-inch baking dish with butter. Arrange bread slices in dish, fitting slices in tightly.

2. Combine eggs, milk, pumpkin, vanilla, pumpkin pie spice and salt in medium bowl; beat until well blended. Pour over bread in prepared baking dish; turn slices to coat completely. Cover and refrigerate 8 hours or overnight.

3. Preheat oven to 350°F. Combine sugar and cinnamon in small bowl; mix well. Turn bread slices again; sprinkle generously with cinnamon-sugar.

4. Bake about 30 minutes or until bread is puffy and golden brown. Serve immediately with maple syrup.

BREAKFAST AND BRUNCH

Raisin-Nut Oatmeal

Makes 4 servings

3¾ cups water

2⅔ cups old-fashioned oats

⅔ cup raisins

½ cup sliced almonds, toasted*

⅓ cup palm sugar or packed brown sugar

½ teaspoon salt

½ teaspoon ground cinnamon

⅛ teaspoon ground ginger

To toast almonds, spread in single layer in small heavy skill. Cook over medium heat 2 to 3 minutes or until nuts are lightly browned, stirring frequently. Cool before using.

1. Bring water to a boil in large saucepan over high heat. Stir in remaining ingredients.

2. Reduce heat to medium. Cook and stir 4 to 5 minutes or until thick and creamy.

NOTE: For richer oatmeal, substitute 2 cups milk for 2 cups of the water.

Oatmeal Waffles with Spiced Apple Compote

Makes 6 servings

APPLE COMPOTE

- 2 **tablespoons butter**
- 1 **pound Granny Smith apples, peeled and cut into ½-inch pieces**
- ¼ **cup maple syrup**
- ½ **cup water**
- ¼ **cup raisins**
- 1 **teaspoon ground cinnamon**

WAFFLES

- 1¼ **cups quick-cooking oats**
- ¾ **cup oat flour**
- ¼ **cup ground flaxseed**
- 1 **tablespoon baking powder**
- ½ **teaspoon salt**
- 1¾ **cups milk, heated**
- ½ **cup (1 stick) butter, melted and cooled slightly**
- 3 **eggs**
- ¼ **cup maple syrup**

1. Preheat oven to 200°F. Set wire rack on top of large baking sheet; place in oven.

2. For compote, melt 2 tablespoons butter in large nonstick skillet over medium-high heat. Add apples, ¼ cup maple syrup, water, raisins and cinnamon; mix well. Reduce heat to medium. Cover and cook 5 minutes. Uncover; continue cooking 5 minutes or until apples are tender and most of liquid has evaporated, stirring occasionally. Set aside.

3. For waffles, combine oats, flour, flaxseed, baking powder and salt in large bowl. Pour in hot milk; stir until combined. Let stand 5 minutes.

4. Whisk melted butter, eggs and ¼ cup maple syrup in medium bowl. Pour into oat mixture; stir until combined.

5. Preheat Belgium waffle maker to medium-high heat. Pour ⅓ cup batter into each well of waffle maker. Close lid; cook 6 minutes or until golden brown. Remove waffles to wire rack in oven; tent with foil to keep warm. Repeat with remaining batter.

6. Serve waffles with apple compote.

BREAKFAST AND BRUNCH

Garden Vegetable Muffins

Makes 12 muffins

2 cups all-purpose flour

2 tablespoons sugar

1 tablespoon baking powder

¼ teaspoon salt

3 ounces cream cheese

¾ cup milk

½ cup finely shredded or grated carrots

¼ cup chopped green onions

¼ cup vegetable oil

1 egg

1. Preheat oven to 400°F. Grease 12 standard (2½-inch) muffin cups or line with paper baking cups.

2. Combine flour, sugar, baking powder and salt in large bowl. Cut in cream cheese with pastry blender or two knives until mixture resembles coarse crumbs.

3. Combine milk, carrots, green onions, oil and egg in small bowl until blended. Stir into flour mixture just until moistened. Spoon evenly into prepared muffin cups.

4. Bake 25 to 30 minutes until toothpick inserted into centers comes out clean.

5. Immediately remove from pan. Cool on wire rack 10 minutes. Serve warm.

FRESH SALADS

Italian Bread Salad

Makes 4 servings

1. Preheat oven to 400°F. Spread bread cubes on baking sheet. Bake 5 to 7 minutes or until lightly toasted and dry, stirring occasionally. Remove to bowl; let cool.

2. Whisk buttermilk, garlic, dill, onion powder, ¼ teaspoon salt and pepper in small bowl until well blended. Let stand 15 minutes to allow flavors to blend.

3. Spoon equal amounts of bread cubes into bottom of four (1-pint) resealable jars. Layer tomatoes, cucumber, celery and basil over bread. Sprinkle with additional salt, if desired.

4. Stir dressing; pour equal amounts over salads. Seal jars; shake to distribute dressing. Refrigerate until ready to serve.

4 slices Italian bread, cut into ½-inch cubes (about 4 cups)

½ cup buttermilk

1 clove garlic, minced

1 tablespoon minced fresh dill or 1 teaspoon dried dill weed

1½ teaspoons onion powder

¼ teaspoon salt, plus additional as needed

¼ teaspoon black pepper

½ cup cherry or grape tomatoes, quartered

1 cucumber, peeled, cut in half lengthwise, seeded and thinly sliced

1 stalk celery, thinly sliced

2 tablespoons minced fresh basil

FRESH SALADS

Warm Brussels Sprouts Salad with Mustard Vinaigrette

Makes 4 servings

- 3 cups brussels sprouts, cut into quarters
- 1 pint (2 cups) grape tomatoes
- ½ cup sliced red onion
- 3 tablespoons olive oil, divided
- 2 tablespoons balsamic vinegar, divided
- ¼ teaspoon salt
- 1 tablespoon water
- 2 teaspoons Dijon mustard
- 1 teaspoon honey
- 4 cups chopped butter lettuce
- ¼ cup shaved Parmesan cheese

1. Preheat oven to 375°F.

2. Combine brussels sprouts, tomatoes and onion in large bowl. Add 1 tablespoon oil, 1 tablespoon vinegar and salt; toss to coat evenly. Arrange in single layer on baking sheet.

3. Bake 20 minutes or until brussels sprouts are browned and tender, stirring once. Let stand 10 minutes to cool slightly.

4. Meanwhile, whisk remaining 2 tablespoons oil, 1 tablespoon vinegar, water, mustard and honey in large bowl until smooth and well blended. Add vegetables; toss to coat evenly.

5. Arrange lettuce on 4 plates. Spoon vegetables evenly over lettuce. Top with cheese.

VEGAN: Omit Parmesan cheese and substitute agave nectar or maple syrup for the honey.

FRESH SALADS

Coleslaw

Makes 10 servings

1 medium head green cabbage, shredded

1 medium carrot, shredded

½ cup mayonnaise

½ cup milk

⅓ cup sugar

3 tablespoons lemon juice

1½ tablespoons white vinegar

½ teaspoon salt

⅛ teaspoon black pepper

1. Combine cabbage and carrot in large bowl; mix well.

2. Combine mayonnaise, milk, sugar, lemon juice, vinegar, salt and pepper in medium bowl; whisk until well blended. Add to cabbage mixture; stir until blended.

3. Cover and refrigerate at least 1 hour before serving for flavors to blend.

NF Q GF EF MA

FRESH SALADS

Superfood Kale Salad

Makes 4 servings

MAPLE-ROASTED CARROTS

- 8 **carrots, trimmed**
- 2 **tablespoons maple syrup**
- 2 **tablespoons olive oil**
- ½ **teaspoon salt**
- ⅛ **teaspoon black pepper**
- Dash **ground red pepper**

VINAIGRETTE

- ¼ **cup extra virgin olive oil**
- 2 **tablespoons maple syrup**
- 3 **tablespoons lemon juice**
- ¾ **teaspoon grated lemon peel**
- ½ **teaspoon salt**
- ⅛ **teaspoon black pepper**

SALAD

- 4 **cups chopped kale**
- 2 **cups chopped mixed greens**
- 1 **cup dried cranberries**
- 1 **cup slivered almonds, toasted***
- 1 **cup shredded Parmesan cheese**

*To toast almonds, spread on ungreased baking sheet. Bake in preheated 350°F oven 6 to 8 minutes or until lightly browned, stirring occasionally.

1. Preheat oven to 400°F. Line baking sheet with parchment paper. Spray 13×9-inch baking pan with nonstick cooking spray.

2. Place carrots on prepared baking sheet. Whisk 2 tablespoons maple syrup, 2 tablespoons oil, ½ teaspoon salt, ⅛ teaspoon black pepper and red pepper in small bowl until well blended. Brush some of oil mixture over carrots. Roast 30 minutes or until carrots are tender, brushing with oil mixture and shaking pan every 10 minutes. Slice crosswise into coins when carrots are cool enough to handle.

3. While carrots are roasting, prepare vinaigrette. Whisk ¼ cup oil, 2 tablespoons maple syrup, lemon juice, lemon peel, ½ teaspoon salt and ⅛ teaspoon black pepper in small bowl until well blended.

4. Combine kale, greens, cranberries, almonds and cheese in large bowl. Add carrots. Pour vinaigrette over salad; toss to coat.

VEGAN: Omit Parmesan cheese.

MAKE AHEAD: Substitute additional kale for the spring greens or plan on adding the spring greens just before serving. Kale stands up well to being dressed ahead of time, whereas spring greens get soft very quickly.

GF EF MA

FRESH SALADS

Asparagus and Arugula Salad

Makes 4 to 6 servings

- ½ cup sun-dried tomatoes (not packed in oil)
- 1 cup boiling water
- 1 cup sliced asparagus (1-inch pieces)
- 1 package (5 ounces) baby arugula (4 cups)
- ½ cup shaved Parmesan cheese
- ¼ cup extra virgin olive oil
- 2 tablespoons lemon juice
- 1 tablespoon orange juice
- 1 clove garlic, minced
- ½ teaspoon salt
- ½ teaspoon grated lemon peel
- ⅛ teaspoon black pepper (optional)

1. Place sun-dried tomatoes in small bowl; pour boiling water over tomatoes. Let stand 5 minutes; drain well.

2. Bring medium saucepan of salted water to a boil. Add asparagus; cook 1 minute or until crisp-tender. Rinse under cold water to stop cooking.

3. Combine arugula, asparagus, sun-dried tomatoes and cheese in large bowl. Whisk oil, lemon juice, orange juice, garlic, salt, lemon peel and pepper, if desired, in small bowl until well blended. Pour over salad; toss gently to coat.

VEGAN: Omit Parmesan cheese.

FRESH SALADS

Cabbage and Red Potato Salad with Cilantro-Lime Dressing

Makes 4 servings

12 ounces baby red potatoes, quartered and cooked

¾ teaspoon salt, divided

½ cup finely chopped fresh cilantro

2 tablespoons lime juice

2 tablespoons extra virgin olive oil

2 teaspoons maple syrup

½ teaspoon ground cumin

2 cups sliced napa cabbage

2 cups sliced red cabbage

½ cup sliced green onions

2 tablespoons unsalted sunflower kernels

1. Place potatoes in medium saucepan. Add water to cover and ½ teaspoon salt. Bring to a boil. Reduce heat; simmer 10 to 15 minutes or until potatoes are tender. Drain and rinse under cold water to stop cooking.

2. Whisk cilantro, lime juice, oil, maple syrup, cumin and remaining ¼ teaspoon salt in small bowl until smooth and well blended. Let stand 30 minutes to allow flavors to blend.

3. Combine napa cabbage, red cabbage, potatoes and green onions in large bowl; mix well. Add dressing; toss to coat evenly. Sprinkle with sunflower kernels just before serving.

FRESH SALADS

Spinach Salad with Goat Cheese-Stuffed Mushrooms and Shallot Vinaigrette

Makes 4 servings

¼ cup extra virgin olive oil

3 tablespoons balsamic vinegar

2 teaspoons finely chopped shallots

¼ teaspoon salt

8 large cremini mushrooms

2 teaspoons honey

4 ounces herbed goat cheese, softened

2 tablespoons cream cheese, softened

5 ounces baby spinach *or* 1 bunch spinach

¼ cup sliced or slivered toasted almonds*

*To toast almonds, spread on ungreased baking sheet. Bake in preheated 350°F oven 6 to 8 minutes or until lightly browned, stirring frequently.

1. Whisk oil, vinegar, shallots and salt in small bowl until well blended. Remove stems from mushrooms. Place mushrooms on large plate, gill side up. Drizzle with 2 tablespoons dressing; let stand 15 to 30 minutes. Whisk honey into remaining dressing; set aside.

2. Preheat oven to 400°F. Combine goat cheese and cream cheese in small bowl.

3. Place mushrooms in baking dish, gill side down. Bake 10 minutes. Turn mushrooms over; fill each mushroom with about 1 tablespoon goat cheese mixture. Bake 5 to 10 minutes or until cheese is warm and soft.

4. Arrange spinach on 4 serving plates.

5. Remove mushrooms from baking dish. Pour cooking liquid into dressing. Pour half of dressing over spinach; toss to coat. Arrange mushrooms on salad; drizzle with remaining dressing. Sprinkle with almonds.

FRESH SALADS

DRESSING

- ¼ **cup balsamic vinegar**
- 1 **clove garlic, minced**
- ½ **teaspoon sugar**
- ¼ **teaspoon salt**
- ⅛ **teaspoon black pepper**
- ¼ **cup extra virgin olive oil**
- ¼ **cup vegetable oil**

SALAD

- 8 **cups packed baby spinach**
- 1 **cup diced tomatoes**
- 1 **cup drained mandarin oranges**
- 1 **cup glazed pecans***
- ½ **cup crumbled feta cheese**
- ½ **cup diced red onion**
- ½ **cup dried cranberries**
- 1 **can (3 ounces) crispy rice noodles****
- 4 **teaspoons toasted sesame seeds**

Glazed pecans can be found in the produce section of many supermarkets (with other salad toppings). Or make them yourself. (See Tip.)

**Crispy rice noodles can be found with canned chow mein noodles in the Asian section of the supermarket.*

Spinach Salad

Makes 4 servings

1. For dressing, whisk vinegar, garlic, sugar, salt and pepper in medium bowl until blended. Whisk in olive oil and vegetable oil in thin steady stream until well blended.

2. Divide spinach among 4 serving bowls. Top evenly with tomatoes, oranges, pecans, cheese, onion and cranberries. Sprinkle with rice noodles and sesame seeds. Drizzle each salad with 3 tablespoons dressing.

TIP: To make glazed pecans, combine 1 cup pecan halves, ¼ cup sugar, 1 tablespoon butter and ½ teaspoon salt in medium skillet; cook and stir over medium heat 5 minutes or until sugar mixture is dark brown and nuts are well coated. Spread on large plate; cool completely. Break into pieces or coarsely chop.

VEGAN: Omit cheese.

FRESH SALADS

Beet and Arugula Salad

Makes 4 servings

- 3 **medium beets, trimmed**
- 6 **cups baby arugula**
- 2 **tablespoons chopped shallots**
- 1 **tablespoon white wine vinegar**
- 1 **teaspoon Dijon mustard**
- ¼ **teaspoon salt**
- ⅛ **teaspoon black pepper**
- 3 **tablespoons extra virgin olive oil**
- 4 **wedges (1 ounce each) aged Irish Cheddar cheese**

1. Place beets in medium saucepan; add cold water to cover by 2 inches. Bring to a boil over medium-high heat; cook 35 to 40 minutes or until beets can be easily pierced with tip of knife. Drain beets; cool 15 minutes.

2. Peel beets; cut into ½-inch cubes. Transfer to medium bowl. Place arugula in separate medium bowl. Combine shallots, vinegar, mustard, salt and pepper in small bowl. Slowly whisk in oil until well blended. Toss beets with 1 tablespoon dressing. Toss arugula with remaining dressing.

3. Divide arugula among 4 plates. Top with beets; garnish with wedge of cheese. Serve immediately.

VEGAN: Omit cheese.

FRESH SALADS

Taco Salad To Go

Makes 4 (1-quart) jars

DRESSING

- ¼ **cup mayonnaise**
- ¼ **cup plain yogurt or sour cream**
- 1 **tablespoon lime juice**
- ½ **teaspoon chipotle chili powder**
- 1 **clove garlic, minced**
- ¼ **cup crumbled cotija cheese**
- ¼ **cup chopped fresh cilantro**

SALAD

- 1 **tablespoon vegetable oil**
- 1 **package (16 ounces) frozen corn**
- ¼ **teaspoon salt**
- 1 **large avocado, diced**
- 1 **teaspoon lime juice**
- 1 **can (15 ounces) black beans, rinsed and drained**
- 2 **medium tomatoes, seeded and diced**
- ½ **cup finely chopped red onion**
- **Packaged corn tortilla strips or chips**
- **Chopped fresh lettuce or spinach**

1. For dressing, whisk mayonnaise, yogurt, 1 tablespoon lime juice, chili powder and garlic in small bowl. Stir in cheese and cilantro.

2. For salad, heat oil in saucepan over high heat. Add corn; cook 10 to 15 minutes or until lightly browned, stirring occasionally. Stir in salt. Transfer to medium bowl; cool to room temperature. Combine avocado and 1 teaspoon lime juice in small bowl; toss to coat.

3. For each 1-quart jar, layer 2½ tablespoons dressing, ½ cup corn, scant ½ cup black beans, ¼ cup tomatoes, 2 tablespoons onion and about ¼ cup avocado. Top with tortilla strips and lettuce. Seal jars.

4. Refrigerate until ready to serve.

NOTE: You can also make these without the lettuce. If so, use four (1-pint) jars.

NF GF EF MA

FRESH SALADS

Mediterranean Main Salad

Makes 4 servings

1⅓ cups water

⅔ cup uncooked quick-cooking pearl barley

1 can (14 ounces) quartered artichoke hearts, drained and coarsely chopped

2 medium tomatoes, seeded and chopped

¼ cup chopped fresh parsley

1 tablespoon extra virgin olive oil

1 tablespoon Greek seasoning

1 teaspoon grated lemon peel

2 tablespoons lemon juice

1 package (4 ounces) feta cheese, crumbled

1. Bring water to a boil in medium saucepan. Stir in barley. Reduce heat; cover and simmer 10 to 12 minutes or until tender.

2. Meanwhile, combine artichokes, tomatoes, parsley, oil, Greek seasoning, lemon peel and lemon juice in large bowl. Toss gently to blend.

3. Drain barley; rinse under cold water to cool quickly; drain well.

4. Add barley to artichoke mixture; toss well. Add cheese; toss gently to blend.

VEGAN: Omit cheese.

SOUPS AND STEWS

Cream of Asparagus Soup

Makes 6 to 8 servings

1. Trim off and discard tough ends of asparagus. Cut asparagus into 1-inch pieces. Combine asparagus and 1 cup broth in medium saucepan; cook 12 to 15 minutes or until tender.

2. Remove 1 cup asparagus pieces; reserve. Process remaining asparagus pieces with broth in blender or food processor until smooth.

3. Melt butter in large saucepan. Stir in flour until smooth. Gradually add remaining 2½ cups broth; cook until slightly thickened, stirring occasionally. Stir in cream, salt, pepper, asparagus mixture and reserved asparagus pieces; cook until heated through.

1	**pound asparagus**
3½	**cups vegetable broth, divided**
¼	**cup (½ stick) butter**
¼	**cup all-purpose flour**
½	**cup whipping cream or milk**
½	**teaspoon salt**
⅛	**teaspoon black pepper**

Minestrone Soup

Makes 4 to 6 servings

1 tablespoon olive oil

½ cup chopped onion

1 stalk celery, diced

1 carrot, diced

2 cloves garlic, minced

2 cups vegetable broth

1½ cups water

1 bay leaf

¾ teaspoon salt

½ teaspoon dried basil

½ teaspoon dried oregano

¼ teaspoon dried thyme

¼ teaspoon sugar

Black pepper

1 can (15 ounces) dark red kidney beans, rinsed and drained

1 can (15 ounces) navy beans or cannellini beans, rinsed and drained

1 can (about 14 ounces) diced tomatoes

1 cup diced zucchini

½ cup uncooked small shell pasta

½ cup frozen cut green beans

¼ cup dry red wine

1 cup packed chopped fresh spinach

1. Heat oil in large saucepan or Dutch oven over medium-high heat. Add onion, celery, carrot and garlic; cook and stir 5 to 7 minutes or until vegetables are tender. Add broth, water, bay leaf, salt, basil, oregano, thyme, sugar and pepper; bring to a boil.

2. Stir in kidney beans, navy beans, tomatoes, zucchini, pasta, green beans and wine; cook 10 minutes, stirring occasionally.

3. Add spinach; cook 2 minutes or until pasta and zucchini are tender.

GLUTEN-FREE: Use any small shape of gluten-free pasta instead of regular shell pasta.

Rainbow Vegetable Stew

Makes 4 to 6 servings

1 tablespoon olive oil

1 red onion, chopped

2 stalks celery, chopped

3 cloves garlic, minced

2 teaspoons salt, divided

4 cups vegetable broth

1 butternut squash (about 2 pounds) peeled and cut into ½-inch cubes

1 red bell pepper, chopped

1 green bell pepper, chopped

1 teaspoon ground cumin

½ teaspoon dried oregano

¼ teaspoon chipotle chili powder

¾ cup uncooked tricolor or white quinoa

1½ cups water

½ cup corn

1 can (15 ounces) black beans, rinsed and drained

½ cup chopped fresh parsley

1 tablespoon lime juice

1. Heat oil in large saucepan over medium-high heat. Add onion and celery; cook and stir 5 minutes or until vegetables are softened. Add garlic and 1½ teaspoons salt; cook and stir 30 seconds. Stir in broth, squash, bell peppers, cumin, oregano and chili powder; bring to a boil. Reduce heat to medium; simmer 20 minutes or until squash is tender.

2. Rinse quinoa in fine mesh strainer under cold water. Meanwhile, bring 1½ cups water, quinoa and remaining ½ teaspoon salt to a boil in medium saucepan. Reduce heat to low; cover and simmer 15 minutes or until quinoa is tender and water is absorbed.

3. Stir corn and beans into stew; cook 5 minutes or until heated through. Stir in parsley and lime juice. Serve with quinoa.

SOUPS AND STEWS

Garden Vegetable Soup

Makes 8 to 10 servings

1 tablespoon olive oil

1 medium onion, chopped

1 carrot, chopped

1 stalk celery, chopped

1 medium zucchini, diced

1 medium yellow squash, diced

1 red bell pepper, diced

2 tablespoons tomato paste

2 cloves garlic, minced

2 teaspoons salt

1 teaspoon Italian seasoning

½ teaspoon black pepper

8 cups vegetable broth

1 can (28 ounces) whole tomatoes, chopped, juice reserved

½ cup uncooked pearl barley

1 cup cut green beans (1-inch pieces)

½ cup corn

¼ cup slivered fresh basil

1 tablespoon lemon juice

1. Heat oil in large saucepan or Dutch oven over medium-high heat. Add onion, carrot and celery; cook and stir 8 minutes or until vegetables are softened. Add zucchini, yellow squash and bell pepper; cook and stir 5 minutes or until softened. Stir in tomato paste, garlic, salt, Italian seasoning and black pepper; cook 1 minute. Stir in broth and tomatoes with juice; bring to a boil. Stir in barley.

2. Reduce heat to low; cook 30 minutes. Stir in green beans and corn; cook about 15 minutes or until barley is tender and green beans are crisp-tender. Stir in basil and lemon juice.

Lentil-Barley Soup

Makes 8 servings

- 1 tablespoon olive oil
- ½ cup chopped onion
- ½ cup chopped celery
- 1 teaspoon minced garlic
- 4 cups vegetable broth
- 2 cups water
- 1 can (28 ounces) diced tomatoes
- ¾ cup uncooked pearl barley
- ¾ cup dried lentils, rinsed and sorted
- 1 tablespoon fresh oregano *or* 1 teaspoon dried oregano
- 1½ teaspoons fresh rosemary *or* ½ teaspoon dried rosemary
- 1 teaspoon lemon-pepper seasoning
- 1 cup thinly sliced carrots
- 1 cup (4 ounces) shredded Swiss or mozzarella cheese

1. Heat oil in large saucepan over medium heat. Add onion and celery; cook and stir 5 minutes or until softened. Add garlic; cook and stir 30 seconds.

2. Add broth, water, tomatoes, barley, lentils, oregano, rosemary and lemon-pepper seasoning. Bring to a boil over high heat. Reduce heat; cover and simmer 45 minutes or until barley and lentils are tender, stirring occasionally.

3. Add carrots; cover and simmer 15 minutes or until carrots are tender and soup is thickened. Sprinkle with cheese just before serving.

VEGAN: Omit cheese.

Broccoli Cheese Soup

Makes 4 to 6 servings (7 cups)

6 tablespoons (¾ stick) butter

1 cup chopped onion

1 clove garlic, minced

¼ cup all-purpose flour

2 cups vegetable broth

2 cups milk

1½ teaspoons Dijon mustard

½ teaspoon salt

¼ teaspoon ground nutmeg

¼ teaspoon black pepper

⅛ teaspoon hot pepper sauce

1 package (16 ounces) frozen broccoli (5 cups)

2 carrots, shredded (1 cup)

6 ounces pasteurized process cheese product, cubed

1 cup (4 ounces) shredded sharp Cheddar cheese, plus additional for garnish

1. Melt butter in large saucepan or Dutch oven over medium-low heat. Add onion; cook and stir 10 minutes or until softened. Add garlic; cook and stir 1 minute. Increase heat to medium. Whisk in flour until smooth; cook and stir 3 minutes without browning.

2. Gradually whisk in broth and milk. Add mustard, salt, nutmeg, black pepper and hot pepper sauce; cook 15 minutes or until thickened.

3. Add broccoli; cook 15 minutes. Add carrots; cook 10 minutes or until vegetables are tender.

4. Transfer half of soup to food processor or blender; process until smooth. Return to saucepan. Add cheese product and 1 cup Cheddar; cook and stir over low heat until cheese is melted. Ladle into bowls; garnish with additional Cheddar.

Italian Escarole and White Bean Stew

Makes 4 servings

1 tablespoon olive oil

1 onion, chopped

3 carrots, cut into ½-inch-thick rounds

2 cloves garlic, minced

1 can (about 14 ounces) vegetable broth

1 head escarole (about 12 ounces)

¼ teaspoon red pepper flakes

2 cans (about 15 ounces each) Great Northern white beans, rinsed and drained

Salt

Grated Parmesan cheese (optional)

SLOW COOKER DIRECTIONS

1. Heat oil in medium skillet over medium-high heat. Add onion and carrots; cook and stir about 5 minutes or until onion is softened. Add garlic; cook and stir 1 minute. Transfer to slow cooker. Pour in broth.

2. Trim base of escarole. Roughly cut crosswise into 1-inch-wide strips. Wash well in large bowl of cold water. Lift out by handfuls, leaving sand or dirt in bottom of bowl. Shake to remove excess water, but do not dry. Add to slow cooker. Sprinkle with red pepper flakes. Top with beans.

3. Cover; cook on LOW 7 to 8 hours or on HIGH 3½ to 4 hours or until escarole is wilted and very tender. Season with salt. Serve in bowls and sprinkle with Parmesan, if desired.

TIP: Escarole is very leafy and easily fills a 4½-quart slow cooker when raw, but it shrinks dramatically as it cooks down. This recipe makes 4 portions, but can easily be doubled. Simply double the quantities of all the ingredients listed and be sure to use a 6-quart (or larger) slow cooker.

VEGAN: Omit cheese.

Barley Stew with Cornmeal-Cheese Dumplings

Makes 4 servings

STEW

- 2 **cans (11½ ounces each) spicy vegetable juice cocktail**
- 1 **can (15 ounces) butter beans, drained**
- 1 **can (about 14 ounces) stewed tomatoes, undrained**
- 1 **cup sliced zucchini**
- 1 **cup sliced carrots**
- 1 **cup water**
- ½ **cup chopped peeled parsnip**
- ⅓ **cup quick pearl barley**
- 1 **bay leaf**
- 2 **tablespoons chopped fresh thyme**
- 1½ **tablespoons chopped fresh rosemary leaves**
- ½ **teaspoon salt**

DUMPLINGS

- ⅓ **cup all-purpose flour**
- ⅓ **cup cornmeal**
- 1 **teaspoon baking powder**
- ¼ **cup milk**
- 1 **tablespoon canola oil**
- ⅓ **cup (1½ ounces) shredded Cheddar cheese**

1. Combine vegetable juice, beans, tomatoes with juice, zucchini, carrots, water, parsnip, barley, bay leaf, thyme and rosemary in large saucepan. Bring to a boil over high heat. Reduce heat to medium-low. Cover; simmer 20 to 25 minutes or until tender, stirring occasionally. Remove and discard bay leaf.

2. Combine flour, cornmeal and baking powder in small bowl. Combine milk and oil in separate small bowl; stir into flour mixture. Stir in cheese. Drop dough by spoonfuls to make 4 mounds onto boiling stew. Cover; simmer 10 to 12 minutes or until wooden toothpick inserted near center of dumpling comes out clean.

SOUPS AND STEWS

Curried Ginger Pumpkin Soup

Makes 8 servings

1 tablespoon vegetable oil

1 large sweet onion, coarsely chopped

1 large Golden Delicious apple, peeled and coarsely chopped

3 slices (¼-inch) peeled fresh ginger

1½ teaspoons curry powder

2½ to 3 cups vegetable broth, divided

2 cans (15 ounces each) pumpkin puree

1 cup canned coconut milk

1 teaspoon salt

Black pepper

Roasted salted pumpkin seeds (pepitas)

1. Heat oil in large saucepan over medium heat. Add onion, apple, ginger and curry powder; cook and stir 10 minutes. Add ½ cup broth; cover and simmer 10 minutes or until apple is tender.

2. Pour onion mixture into blender; blend until smooth. Return to saucepan. (Or use hand-held immersion blender.)

3. Add pumpkin, 2 cups broth, coconut milk, salt and pepper; cook until heated through, stirring occasionally. If soup is too thick, add additional broth, a few tablespoons at a time, until soup reaches desired consistency. Sprinkle with pumpkin seeds, if desired.

SMALL PLATES

Mediterranean Baked Feta

Makes 4 to 6 servings

1. Preheat oven to 400°F.

2. Place cheese in small baking dish; top with tomatoes, roasted peppers and olives. Sprinkle with oregano and season with black pepper; drizzle with oil.

3. Bake 12 minutes or until cheese is soft. Sprinkle with basil. Serve immediately with pita chips.

GLUTEN-FREE: Serve with corn tortilla chips or gluten-free crackers.

1 package (8 ounces) feta cheese, cut crosswise into 4 slices

½ cup grape tomatoes, halved

¼ cup sliced roasted red peppers

¼ cup pitted kalamata olives

⅛ teaspoon dried oregano

Black pepper

2 tablespoons extra virgin olive oil

1 tablespoon shredded fresh basil

Pita chips

SMALL PLATES

Crostini with Lemony Pesto
Makes 16 crostini

1 (4-ounce) French baguette

3 tablespoons prepared pesto

½ teaspoon lemon juice

½ cup chopped plum tomato

1. Preheat oven to 350°F.

2. Cut baguette crosswise into 16 slices; arrange on baking sheet. Bake 11 to 12 minutes or until bread begins to brown. Cool completely.

3. Combine pesto and lemon juice in small bowl; stir until well blended. Spread each bread slice with ½ teaspoon pesto mixture. Top with tomato. Serve immediately.

SMALL PLATES

Cauliflower Tacos with Chipotle Crema

Makes 8 tacos

- 1 package (8 ounces) sliced cremini mushrooms
- 4 tablespoons olive oil, divided
- 1¾ teaspoons salt, divided
- 1 head cauliflower
- 1 teaspoon ground cumin
- ½ teaspoon dried oregano
- ¼ teaspoon ground coriander
- ¼ teaspoon ground cinnamon
- ¼ teaspoon black pepper
- ½ cup vegan sour cream
- 2 teaspoons lime juice
- ½ teaspoon chipotle chili powder
- ½ cup vegetarian refried beans
- 8 taco-size corn tortillas
- Chopped fresh cilantro (optional)
- Pickled Red Onions (recipe follows) or sliced red onion

1. Preheat oven to 400°F. Toss mushrooms with 1 tablespoon oil and ¼ teaspoon salt in large bowl. Spread on small baking sheet.

2. Remove leaves from cauliflower. Remove florets; cut into 1-inch pieces. Place in same large bowl. Add remaining 3 tablespoons oil, 1 teaspoon salt, cumin, oregano, coriander, cinnamon and black pepper; mix well. Spread on sheet pan in single layer.

3. Roast cauliflower about 40 minutes or until browned and tender, stirring a few times. Roast mushrooms 20 minutes or until dry and browned, stirring once.

4. For crema, combine sour cream, lime juice, chili powder and remaining ½ teaspoon salt in small bowl.

5. For each taco, spread 1 tablespoon beans over tortilla; spread 1 teaspoon crema over beans. Top with about 3 mushroom slices and ¼ cup cauliflower. Top with cilantro and red onions, if desired. Fold in half.

PICKLED RED ONIONS: Thinly slice 1 small red onion; place in large glass jar. Add ¼ cup white wine vinegar or distilled white vinegar, 2 tablespoons water, 1 teaspoon sugar and 1 teaspoon salt. Seal jar; shake well. Refrigerate at least 1 hour or up to 1 week. Makes about ½ cup.

NF GF EF V DF

SMALL PLATES

Fried Zucchini

Makes 4 to 6 servings

2 medium zucchini (about 10 ounces each)

¼ cup all-purpose flour

½ teaspoon salt

½ teaspoon dried oregano

1 egg, beaten

½ cup vegetable oil for frying

½ cup panko bread crumbs

½ cup marinara or tomato sauce, heated

1. Trim ends from zucchini; cut in half crosswise. Using spiralizer, spiral zucchini with fine ribbon blade. Pile loosely on cutting board; cut 3 times as if cutting into 6 wedges. Squeeze dry in paper towels if zucchini is very moist. Place in medium bowl. Add flour, salt and oregano; toss until well coated. Add egg; mix until well blended.

2. Heat oil in large skillet over medium-high heat. Place panko in shallow bowl.

3. Working in batches, shape zucchini mixture into 1-inch balls. Place in panko; press panko onto all sides. Place in hot oil. Cook 2 minutes per side or until golden brown.

4. Drain on paper towels. Serve warm with sauce for dipping.

SMALL PLATES

Whole Wheat Flatbread with Herbed Ricotta, Peaches and Arugula

Makes 4 servings

½ cup ricotta cheese

2 tablespoons finely chopped fresh basil

½ teaspoon coarse salt

⅛ teaspoon black pepper

2 whole wheat naan breads

1 ripe peach, cut into 12 slices

½ cup arugula

½ teaspoon lemon juice

1 teaspoon extra virgin olive oil

2 teaspoons balsamic vinegar

Flaky sea salt, for sprinkling

1. Preheat oven to 400°F. Line baking sheet with parchment paper.

2. Combine ricotta cheese, basil, coarse salt and pepper in small bowl. Spread mixture evenly on each piece of naan. Arrange peaches on top. Bake 12 minutes or until bottom of naan is crisp.

3. Combine arugula, lemon juice and oil in medium bowl; toss gently. Top baked flatbreads with arugula. Drizzle with vinegar and sprinkle with sea salt.

4. Cut each flatbread into quarters to serve.

SMALL PLATES

Spanikopita Cups

Makes 16 cups

6 tablespoons (¾ stick) butter, melted

2 eggs

1 container (15 ounces) ricotta cheese

1 package (10 ounces) frozen chopped spinach, thawed and squeezed dry

1 package (4 to 5 ounces) crumbled feta cheese

¾ teaspoon finely grated lemon peel

½ teaspoon salt

¼ teaspoon black pepper

⅛ teaspoon ground nutmeg

8 sheets frozen phyllo dough, thawed

1. Preheat oven to 350°F. Grease 16 standard (2½-inch) muffin pan cups with some of butter.

2. Whisk eggs in large bowl. Add ricotta, spinach, feta, lemon peel, salt, pepper and nutmeg; whisk until well blended.

3. Place one sheet of phyllo on work surface. Brush with some of butter; top with second sheet. Repeat layers twice. Cut stack of phyllo into 8 rectangles; fit rectangles into muffin cups, pressing into bottoms and sides of cups. Repeat with remaining 4 sheets of phyllo and butter. Fill phyllo cups with spinach mixture.

4. Bake about 18 minutes or until phyllo is golden brown and filling is set. Cool in pan 2 minutes; remove to wire rack. Serve warm.

MAKE AHEAD: Cool cups completely and refrigerate. Reheat on baking sheet in the oven or toaster oven until warm.

SMALL PLATES

Simple Bruschetta

Makes 4 servings

1 tablespoon extra virgin olive oil

2 tablespoons thinly sliced red onion

1 clove garlic, minced

1 cup chopped seeded tomato

¼ teaspoon salt

⅛ teaspoon black pepper

Toasted or grilled baguette slices

¼ cup slivered fresh basil

1. Heat oil in medium skillet over medium heat. Add onion; cook and stir 3 minutes. Add garlic; cook and stir 1 minute.

2. Stir in tomato, salt and pepper; let stand 10 minutes. Serve mixture on baguette slices; sprinkle with basil.

MAKE AHEAD: Make tomato mixture ahead of time and let it stand at room temperature for several hours. Do not refrigerate it because the texture of the tomatoes will become mushy.

SMALL PLATES

Cacio e Pepe Cups

Makes 12 cups

8 ounces uncooked spaghetti, broken in half

2 eggs

¼ teaspoon coarsely ground black pepper, plus additional for garnish

¾ cup finely shredded or grated Parmesan cheese, divided

Minced fresh parsley

1. Preheat oven to 350°F. Spray 12 standard (2½-inch) muffin cups with nonstick cooking spray.

2. Cook pasta in large saucepan of boiling salted water until al dente. Drain pasta, reserving about 1 tablespoon cooking water.

3. Meanwhile, whisk eggs and ¼ teaspoon pepper in medium bowl. Stir in ½ cup cheese. Add hot pasta and cooking water; stir until well blended and cheese is melted. Divide spaghetti among prepared muffin cups (tongs work best); pour any remaining egg mixture from bowl into cups. Sprinkle tops with remaining ¼ cup cheese and additional pepper.

4. Bake 15 minutes or until tops are set, no longer shiny and lightly browned. Immediately remove from pan. Sprinkle with parsley; serve warm.

GLUTEN-FREE: Use gluten-free spaghetti or other another long shape in place of the regular spaghetti.

SMALL PLATES

Nachos

Makes 8 servings

- 8 (6-inch) corn tortillas
- 2 teaspoons vegetable oil
- 1 cup chopped onion
- 1 tablespoon chili powder
- 2 teaspoons dried oregano
- 1 can (15 ounces) pinto beans or black beans, rinsed and drained
- 1¼ cups (5 ounces) shredded Monterey Jack cheese
- ¾ cup frozen corn, thawed, drained
- 1 jar (2 ounces) pimientos, drained
- 3 tablespoons sliced black olives
- 2 to 3 tablespoons pickled jalapeño pepper slices, drained

1. Preheat oven to 375°F. Sprinkle 1 tortilla with water to dampen; shake off excess water. Repeat with remaining tortillas. Cut each tortilla into 6 wedges. Arrange wedges in single layer on baking sheet. Bake 4 minutes. Rotate sheet. Bake another 2 to 4 minutes or until chips are firm; do not let brown. Remove chips to ovenproof plate to cool. Set aside.

2. Heat oil in medium saucepan over medium-high heat. Add onion; cook and stir 8 to 10 minutes or until tender and beginning to brown. Add chili powder and oregano; stir 1 minute.

3. Remove from heat. Add beans and 2 tablespoons water; mash with fork or potato masher until well blended, leaving some beans whole. Return to heat. Cover and cook 6 to 8 minutes or until bubbly and heated through, stirring occasionally. Stir in additional water if beans become dry. Remove from heat.

4. Sprinkle cheese evenly over chips. Spoon beans over chips.

5. Combine corn and pimientos in small bowl; spoon over beans. Bake about 8 minutes or until cheese melts. Sprinkle with olives and jalapeños.

VEGAN: Use a vegan cheese alternative instead of the Monterey Jack cheese.

SMALL PLATES

Margherita Crostini

Makes 16 appetizers

1 (4-ounce) whole
   wheat mini baguette

4 plum tomatoes

1 cup (4 ounces)
   shredded mozzarella
   cheese

3 tablespoons pesto
   sauce

1. Preheat oven to 400°F. Slice baguette into 16 very thin, diagonal slices. Slice each tomato lengthwise into 4 (¼-inch) slices.

2. Place baguette slices on ungreased baking sheet. Top each with 1 tablespoon cheese and 1 tomato slice.

3. Bake 8 minutes or until bread is lightly toasted and cheese is melted. Top each crostini with about ½ teaspoon pesto sauce. Serve warm.

PASTA AND GRAINS

Spaghetti and Beets Aglio e Olio

Makes 6 servings

1. Using spiralizer, spiral beets with fine spiral blade; cut into desired lengths. Cook spaghetti according to package directions. Drain and return to saucepan, reserving ½ cup water; keep warm. Meanwhile, spray large nonstick skillet with nonstick cooking spray; heat over medium-high heat. Add beets; cook and stir 8 to 10 minutes or until tender.

2. Heat 1 tablespoon oil in large skillet over medium heat. Add bread crumbs; cook 4 to 5 minutes or until golden brown, stirring frequently. Transfer to small bowl.

3. Add remaining ⅓ cup oil, garlic, salt, if desired, and red pepper flakes to same skillet; cook about 3 minutes or until garlic just begins to brown on edges.

4. Add pasta, beets and parsley to skillet; toss to coat with oil mixture. Add some of reserved pasta water to moisten pasta, if desired. Stir in bread crumbs and ½ cup cheese. Top with remaining ¼ cup cheese just before serving.

GLUTEN-FREE: Omit bread crumbs and use gluten-free spaghetti instead of regular.

VEGAN: Omit Parmesan cheese.

- 2 **medium beets, peeled**
- 8 **ounces uncooked spaghetti or thin spaghetti**
- ⅓ **cup plus 1 tablespoon olive oil, divided**
- 1 **cup fresh Italian or French bread crumbs***
- 4 **cloves garlic, very thinly sliced**
- ¾ **teaspoon salt (optional)**
- ½ **teaspoon red pepper flakes**
- ½ **cup chopped fresh Italian parsley**
- ¾ **cup shredded Parmesan cheese, divided**

*To make fresh bread crumbs, tear 2 ounces bread into pieces; process in food processor until coarse crumbs form.

Margherita Pizza with Quinoa Crust

Makes 4 servings

1 cup uncooked quinoa

⅓ cup water, plus additional for soaking

1 teaspoon baking powder

¾ teaspoon kosher salt

1 tablespoon olive oil, plus drizzle for serving

½ cup marinara sauce

1 ball (8 ounces) fresh mozzarella cheese, cut into ¼-inch-thick slices

Fresh basil leaves, flaky sea salt and freshly ground black pepper (optional)

1. Place quinoa in medium bowl; cover with 1 inch of water. Cover bowl; let soak 8 hours or overnight at room temperature. Rinse well and drain.

2. Combine soaked quinoa, ⅓ cup water, baking powder and salt in bowl of food processor. Process 2 minutes or until completely smooth, stopping occasionally to scrape down sides of bowl as needed.

3. Preheat oven to 450°F. Line bottom of 10-inch springform pan with foil. Brush with 1 tablespoon oil. Attach sides of pan. Pour quinoa mixture in pan, using spatula to spread over bottom. Bake 10 to 12 minutes or until quinoa is golden on sides and bottom.

4. Remove pan from oven. Remove sides of pan. Spread marinara sauce evenly over crust. Top with cheese. Bake 10 minutes or until cheese is melted and bottom of crust is golden brown.

5. Slide pizza onto large cutting board. Top with basil; drizzle with additional oil. Sprinkle with sea salt and pepper, if desired. Serve immediately.

PASTA AND GRAINS

Spinach and Feta Farro Stuffed Peppers

Makes 6 servings

1 tablespoon olive oil

1 package (5 ounces) baby spinach

½ cup sliced green onions

2 cloves garlic, minced

1 tablespoon chopped fresh oregano

1 cup farro, cooked according to package directions

1½ cups finely chopped seeded fresh tomatoes

½ teaspoon salt

⅛ teaspoon black pepper

1 container (4 ounces) crumbled feta cheese, divided

3 large bell peppers, halved lengthwise and cored

1. Preheat oven to 350°F.

2. Heat oil in large skillet over medium-high heat. Add spinach, green onions, garlic and oregano; cook 3 minutes, stirring frequently. Stir in farro, tomatoes, salt, black pepper and ½ cup cheese.

3. Spoon farro mixture into bell pepper halves (about ¾ cup each); place in shallow baking pan. Pour ¼ cup water into bottom of pan; cover with foil.

4. Bake 30 minutes or until bell peppers are crisp-tender and filling is heated through. Sprinkle with remaining cheese.

MAKE AHEAD: Make farro mixture ahead of time and stuff in peppers. Place in pan and cover with plastic wrap. Before baking, add ¼ cup water to the pan and cover the pan with foil.

PASTA AND GRAINS

Soba Miso Bowl

Makes 4 servings

PICKLED CARROTS

- **4 carrots, peeled and shredded or julienned**
- **¼ cup water**
- **¼ cup coarsely chopped ginger (½-inch pieces)**
- **2 tablespoons honey**
- **1 tablespoon salt**
- **½ cup rice vinegar**

MISO DRESSING

- **¼ cup vegetable or peanut oil**
- **2 tablespoons white miso paste**
- **2 tablespoons rice vinegar**
- **2 teaspoons grated fresh ginger**
- **2 teaspoons honey**
- **1 teaspoon dark sesame oil**

BOWLS

- **1 to 2 broccoli crowns, cut into florets**
- **6 ounces uncooked soba noodles**
- **2 cups chopped or shredded red cabbage**
- **Sesame seeds and sprouts (optional)**

1. Place carrots in 1-quart jar or medium bowl. Combine ¼ cup water, chopped ginger, 2 tablespoons honey and salt in small saucepan. Cook and stir over medium heat until salt and honey are dissolved. Pour over carrots. Add ½ cup vinegar. Seal jar; shake to blend. Let stand at room temperature at least 30 minutes or refrigerate until ready to use.

2. For dressing, whisk vegetable oil, miso, 2 tablespoons vinegar, grated ginger, 2 teaspoons honey and sesame oil in small bowl.

3. Bring large saucepan of water to a boil. Add broccoli; cook 3 minutes or until desired doneness. Remove from water with slotted spoon; place in medium bowl. Return water to a boil. Add noodles; reduce heat to medium-low. Cook 3 minutes. Drain in colander; rinse under cold water until cool.

4. For each serving, place noodles, cabbage, broccoli and carrots in bowl. Drizzle with dressing. Garnish with sesame seeds and sprouts.

VEGAN: Replace honey with agave nectar or maple syrup.

PASTA AND GRAINS

Three-Cheese Macaroni and Quinoa

Makes 4 servings

- 4 tablespoons (½ stick) butter, divided
- ½ cup panko bread crumbs
- 2 quarts water
- 1 teaspoon salt, divided
- 1½ cups uncooked whole grain elbow macaroni
- ½ cup uncooked quinoa
- 2 tablespoons all-purpose flour
- 1 cup milk
- 1 cup (4 ounces) shredded sharp Cheddar cheese
- 1 cup (4 ounces) shredded Monterey Jack cheese
- ¼ cup grated Parmesan cheese

1. Melt 2 tablespoons butter in medium saucepan over medium heat. Add panko; cook and stir 1 to 2 minutes or until golden. Place in small bowl; set aside.

2. Combine water and ½ teaspoon salt in large saucepan; bring to a boil over high heat. Stir in macaroni and quinoa; cook 10 minutes or until pasta is tender. Drain in fine-mesh strainer. Place in large serving bowl.

3. Melt remaining 2 tablespoons butter in saucepan over medium heat. Whisk in flour; cook 1 minute without browning. Gradually whisk in milk and remaining ½ teaspoon salt; cook 5 minutes or until very thick. Stir in Cheddar and Monterey Jack cheeses until melted. Pour over macaroni mixture.

4. Top with Parmesan cheese and panko.

PASTA AND GRAINS

Greek Salad Bowl

Makes 4 servings

1 cup uncooked pearled farro

2½ cups water

1¼ teaspoons dried oregano or Greek seasoning, divided

½ teaspoon salt, divided

¼ cup extra virgin olive oil

2 tablespoons red wine vinegar

1 clove garlic, minced

⅛ teaspoon black pepper (optional)

2 cucumbers, julienned, cubed or thinly sliced

½ red onion, thinly sliced

2 medium tomatoes, diced

1 can (15 ounces) chickpeas, rinsed and drained

4 ounces feta cheese, cubed or crumbled

1. Rinse farro under cold water; place in medium saucepan. Add 2½ cups water, 1 teaspoon oregano and ¼ teaspoon salt. Bring to a boil over high heat. Reduce heat to medium-low; simmer, uncovered, 20 minutes or until farro is tender. Drain any additional water.

2. Whisk oil, vinegar, garlic, remaining ¼ teaspoon salt, remaining ¼ teaspoon oregano and pepper, if desired, in small bowl.

3. Divide farro among 4 bowls; arrange cucumber, onion, tomatoes, chickpeas and feta around farro. Drizzle with dressing.

MAKE-AHEAD: This bowl is a great make-ahead option for lunches or future dinners. Add some grilled chicken or lamb for a heartier meal, or mix everything together and serve it as a side dish.

NOTE: This is a great recipe to use a spiralizer if you have one. Cut the ends off the cucumbers and spiral slice with the thin ribbon blade. Spiral the red onion with the thin ribbon blade and chop into desired pieces.

VEGAN: Omit cheese or substitute with cubed extra firm silken tofu.

PASTA AND GRAINS

Sesame Noodles

Makes 6 to 8 servings

1 package (16 ounces) uncooked spaghetti

6 tablespoons soy sauce

5 tablespoons dark sesame oil

3 tablespoons sugar

3 tablespoons rice vinegar

2 tablespoons vegetable oil

3 cloves garlic, minced

1 teaspoon grated fresh ginger or ginger paste

½ teaspoon sriracha sauce

2 green onions, sliced

1 red bell pepper

1 cucumber

1 carrot

Sesame seeds (optional)

1. Cook spaghetti according to package directions until al dente in large saucepan of boiling salted water. Drain, reserving 1 tablespoon pasta cooking water.

2. Whisk soy sauce, sesame oil, sugar, vinegar, vegetable oil, garlic, ginger, sriracha and reserved pasta water in large bowl. Stir in noodles and green onions. Let stand at least 30 minutes until noodles have cooled to room temperature and most of sauce is absorbed, stirring occasionally.

3. Meanwhile, cut bell pepper into thin strips. Peel cucumber and carrot and shred with julienne peeler into long strands, or cut into thin strips. Stir into noodles. Serve at room temperature or refrigerate until ready to serve. Top with sesame seeds, if desired.

GLUTEN-FREE: Use gluten-free spaghetti instead of regular spaghetti, or use 12 ounces soba noodles cooked according to package directions.

Swiss Chard, Barley and Feta Gratin

Makes 8 servings

⅔ cup uncooked quick-cooking barley

12 cups (about 13 ounces) Swiss chard, ends trimmed and leaves and stems cut crosswise in ½-inch-wide strips

2 cups water

1 can (about 14 ounces) tomatoes, drained

¾ cup (3 ounces) crumbled feta cheese

½ teaspoon dried oregano

¼ teaspoon salt

⅛ teaspoon black pepper

1 tablespoon butter, melted

½ teaspoon garlic powder

⅔ cup fresh whole wheat bread crumbs*

½ cup vegetable broth

To make fresh bread crumbs, tear 1¼ slices bread into pieces; process in food processor until coarse crumbs form.

1. Preheat oven to 375°F. Spray 2-quart casserole with nonstick cooking spray.

2. Cook barley according to package directions.

3. Place Swiss chard in large saucepan. Add water; cover and bring to a boil. Reduce heat and simmer 13 minutes or until tender. Drain.

4. Combine barley, Swiss chard, tomatoes, cheese, oregano, salt and pepper in prepared casserole. Smooth into even layer.

5. Combine butter and garlic powder in small bowl. Add bread crumbs; mix well. Pour broth over gratin; sprinkle evenly with crumb mixture.

6. Bake 20 minutes or until topping is golden brown. Let stand 5 minutes before serving.

1 package (16 ounces) uncooked large elbow macaroni

½ cup (1 stick) butter, divided

¼ cup all-purpose flour

1½ cups milk

1 teaspoon salt, divided

¼ teaspoon ground nutmeg

⅛ teaspoon ground red pepper

2 cups (8 ounces) shredded Cheddar cheese

1 cup (4 ounces) shredded Monterey Jack cheese

1 cup canned pumpkin

1 cup panko bread crumbs

½ cup chopped hazelnuts or walnuts (optional)

⅛ teaspoon dried sage

1 cup (4 ounces) shredded Chihuahua cheese*

If Chihuahua cheese is not available, substitute additional Monterey Jack cheese.

Pumpkin Mac and Cheese
Makes 6 to 8 servings

1. Preheat oven to 350°F. Spray 2-quart baking dish with nonstick cooking spray. Cook macaroni according to package directions until al dente. Drain and return to saucepan; keep warm.

2. Melt ¼ cup butter in medium saucepan over medium-high heat. Whisk in flour until smooth; cook 1 minute without browning, whisking constantly. Gradually whisk in milk in thin steady stream. Add ¾ teaspoon salt, nutmeg and red pepper; cook 2 to 3 minutes or until thickened, stirring frequently. Gradually add Cheddar and Monterey Jack cheeses, stirring until smooth after each addition. Add pumpkin; cook 1 minute or until heated through, stirring constantly. Pour sauce over pasta; stir to coat.

3. Melt remaining ¼ cup butter in small skillet over medium-low heat; cook until golden brown. Remove from heat; stir in panko, hazelnuts, if desired, sage and remaining ¼ teaspoon salt.

4. Spread half of pasta in prepared baking dish; sprinkle with ½ cup Chihuahua cheese. Top with remaining pasta; sprinkle with remaining Chihuahua cheese. Top with panko mixture.

5. Bake 25 to 30 minutes or until topping is golden brown and pasta is heated through.

MAKE AHEAD: Make ahead through step 4. Refrigerate until ready to bake.

PESTO

PESTO

- 2 **cups packed fresh basil leaves***
- 1 **cup walnuts, toasted**
- ½ **cup shredded Parmesan cheese, plus additional for garnish**
- 4 **cloves garlic**
- 1 **teaspoon salt**
- ¼ **teaspoon black pepper**
- ¾ **cup extra virgin olive oil**

PASTA

- 1 **package (16 ounces) uncooked cavatappi pasta**
- 1 **tablespoon extra virgin olive oil**
- 2 **plum tomatoes, diced (1½ cups)**
- 1 **package (8 ounces) sliced mushrooms**
- ¼ **cup dry white wine**
- ¼ **cup vegetable broth**
- ¼ **cup whipping cream**

Or substitute 1 cup packed fresh parsley leaves for half of basil.

Pesto Cavatappi

Makes 4 to 6 servings

1. For pesto, combine basil, walnuts, ½ cup cheese, garlic, salt and pepper in food processor; pulse until coarsely chopped. With motor running, add ¾ cup oil in thin steady stream; process until well blended. Measure 1 cup pesto for pasta; reserve remaining pesto for another use.

2. Cook pasta in large saucepan of boiling salted water according to package directions until al dente. Drain and return to saucepan; keep warm.

3. Meanwhile, heat 1 tablespoon oil in large skillet over medium-high heat. Add tomatoes and mushrooms; cook about 7 minutes or until most of liquid has evaporated, stirring occasionally. Add wine, broth and cream; bring to a boil. Reduce heat to low; cook about 4 minutes or until sauce has thickened slightly. Stir in 1 cup pesto; cook just until heated through.

4. Pour sauce over pasta; stir gently to coat. Divide pasta among serving bowls; garnish with additional cheese.

GLUTEN-FREE: Use any gluten-free pasta shape instead of the regular cavatappi.

PASTA AND GRAINS

Green Bean, Walnut and Blue Cheese Pasta Salad

Makes 8 servings

- 2 **cups uncooked gemelli pasta**
- 2 **cups trimmed halved green beans**
- 3 **tablespoons olive oil**
- 2 **tablespoons white wine vinegar**
- 1 **tablespoon chopped fresh thyme**
- 1 **tablespoon Dijon mustard**
- 1 **tablespoon fresh lemon juice**
- 1 **teaspoon honey**
- ¼ **teaspoon salt**
- ¼ **teaspoon black pepper**
- ½ **cup chopped walnuts, toasted***
- ½ **cup crumbled blue cheese**

* To toast walnuts, spread in single layer in heavy skillet. Cook over medium heat 1 to 2 minutes until nuts are lightly browned, stirring frequently. Remove from skillet immediately. Cool before using.

1. Cook pasta according to package directions, omitting salt. Add green beans during the last 4 minutes of cooking. Drain. Transfer to large bowl.

2. Meanwhile, whisk oil, vinegar, thyme, mustard, lemon juice, honey, salt and pepper in medium bowl until smooth and well blended.

3. Pour dressing over pasta and green beans; toss to coat evenly. Stir in walnuts and cheese. Serve warm or cover and refrigerate until ready to serve.**
**If serving cold, stir walnuts into salad just before serving.

GLUTEN-FREE: Use any gluten-free pasta shape instead of the regular gemelli.

VEGAN: Omit the cheese and substitute agave nectar for the honey.

PASTA AND GRAINS

Vegetarian Rice Noodles

Makes 4 servings

- 8 ounces thin rice noodles (rice vermicelli)
- ½ cup soy sauce
- ⅓ cup sugar
- ¼ cup lime juice
- 2 fresh red Thai chiles *or* 1 large jalapeño pepper, finely chopped
- ¼ cup vegetable oil
- 8 ounces firm tofu, drained and cut into triangles
- 1 jicama (8 ounces), peeled and chopped *or* 1 can (8 ounces) sliced water chestnuts, drained
- 2 medium sweet potatoes (1 pound), peeled and cut into ¼-inch-thick slices
- 2 large leeks, cut into ¼-inch-thick slices
- ¼ cup chopped dry-roasted peanuts
- 2 tablespoons chopped fresh mint
- 2 tablespoons chopped fresh cilantro

1. Place rice noodles in medium bowl. Cover with hot water; let stand 15 minutes or until soft. Drain well; cut into 3-inch lengths.

2. Combine soy sauce, sugar, lime juice and chiles in small bowl until well blended; set aside.

3. Meanwhile, heat oil in large skillet over medium-high heat. Add tofu; cook and stir 4 minutes per side or until golden brown. Remove with slotted spatula to paper towel-lined wire rack.

4. Add jicama to skillet; cook and stir 5 minutes or until lightly browned. Remove to baking sheet. Cook sweet potatoes in batches until tender and browned, turning once. Remove to wire rack. Add leeks; cook and stir 1 minute; remove to wire rack.

5. Stir soy sauce mixture; add to skillet. Heat until sugar dissolves. Add noodles; toss to coat. Gently stir in tofu, vegetables, peanuts, mint and cilantro.

MAKE AHEAD: Leftovers make a great lunch. Have them cold or warm them briefly in the microwave.

Vegetable Penne Italiano

Makes 4 servings

1 tablespoon olive oil

1 red bell pepper, cut into ½-inch pieces

1 green bell pepper, cut into ½-inch pieces

1 medium sweet onion, halved and thinly sliced

3 cloves garlic, minced

2 tablespoons tomato paste

2 teaspoons salt

1 teaspoon sugar

1 teaspoon Italian seasoning

¼ teaspoon black pepper

1 can (28 ounces) Italian plum tomatoes, chopped, juice reserved

8 ounces uncooked penne pasta

Grated Parmesan cheese

Chopped fresh basil

1. Heat oil in large skillet over medium-high heat. Add bell peppers, onion and garlic; cook and stir 8 minutes or until vegetables are crisp-tender.

2. Add tomato paste, salt, sugar, Italian seasoning and black pepper; cook 1 minute. Stir in tomatoes with juice. Reduce heat to medium-low; cook 15 minutes or until vegetables are tender and sauce is thickened.

3. Meanwhile, cook pasta in large saucepan of salted water according to package directions until al dente. Drain pasta; return to saucepan. Add sauce; stir gently to coat. Divide among 4 serving bowls; top with cheese and basil.

VEGAN: Omit cheese and top with nutritional yeast, if desired.

GLUTEN-FREE: Use any gluten-free pasta shape instead of the regular penne.

Farro, Grape and Roasted Carrot Bowl

Makes 4 to 6 servings

- 1 **pound carrots, peeled, trimmed and halved lengthwise**
- 3 **tablespoons extra virgin olive oil, divided**
- 1 **teaspoon salt, divided**
- ½ **teaspoon ground cumin**
- ¼ **teaspoon ground coriander**
- ⅛ **teaspoon ground nutmeg**
- 1 **package (about 2¼ ounces) slivered almonds**
- 2 **cups water**
- 1 **cup farro, rinsed under cold water**
- 2 **tablespoons balsamic vinegar**
  Salt and black pepper
- 1 **cup halved red grapes**
- ¼ **cup minced red onion**
- 4 **cups mixed spring greens**

1. Preheat oven to 375°F. Place carrots on sheet pan. Drizzle with 1 tablespoon oil. Combine ½ teaspoon salt, cumin, coriander and nutmeg in small bowl; sprinkle over carrots. Toss to coat carrots with oil and spices. Arrange cut sides down in single layer.

2. Roast 30 minutes or until carrots are browned and tender, turning once. Place almonds on small baking sheet; bake about 5 minutes or until almonds are toasted, stirring frequently.

3. Meanwhile, bring 2 cups water and remaining ½ teaspoon salt to a boil in medium saucepan. Stir in farro; reduce heat to medium-low. Cover and simmer 20 to 25 minutes or until tender. Drain and place farro in large bowl.

4. Whisk remaining 2 tablespoons oil into vinegar in small bowl; pour over farro. Stir in grapes and onion; season to taste with additional salt and pepper. Cut carrots into 1-inch pieces; add to farro mixture. Place greens in serving bowls; top with farro salad and sprinkle with almonds.

Hearty Veggie Sandwich

Makes 4 servings

1. Preheat oven to 350°F. Combine mushrooms, 1 tablespoon oil, ½ teaspoon salt and pepper in medium bowl; toss to coat. Spread on large rimmed baking sheet. Roast 20 minutes or until mushrooms are dark brown and dry, stirring after 10 minutes. Cool on baking sheet.

2. Meanwhile, heat remaining 1 tablespoon oil in large skillet over medium heat. Add zucchini and remaining ¼ teaspoon salt; cook and stir 5 minutes or until zucchini is tender and lightly browned. Transfer to bowl; wipe out skillet with paper towels.

3. Spread butter over one side of each bread slice; turn over. Spread pesto over 4 slices; spread mayonnaise over remaining 4 slices. Top pesto-covered slices evenly with mushrooms, then spinach, zucchini and cheese. Top with remaining bread slices, mayonnaise side down.

4. Heat same skillet over medium heat. Add sandwiches; cover and cook 2 minutes per side or until bread is toasted, spinach is slightly wilted and cheese is beginning to melt. Cut sandwiches in half; serve immediately.

1 pound cremini mushrooms, stemmed and thinly sliced (⅛-inch slices)

2 tablespoons olive oil, divided

¾ teaspoon salt, divided

¼ teaspoon black pepper

1 medium zucchini, diced (¼-inch pieces, about 2 cups)

3 tablespoons butter, softened

8 slices artisan whole grain bread

¼ cup prepared pesto

¼ cup mayonnaise

2 cups packed baby spinach

4 slices (about 1 ounce each) mozzarella cheese

Curried Quinoa Burgers

Makes 6 servings

½ cup uncooked quinoa, rinsed well in fine-mesh strainer

½ cup red lentils, rinsed well in fine-mesh strainer

1½ cups water

1½ teaspoons coarse salt, divided

3 tablespoons olive oil, divided

1 medium onion, diced

½ cup frozen peas

3 cloves garlic, minced

2 teaspoons curry powder

1 egg

6 gluten-free or regular hamburger buns

Lettuce, sliced tomatoes, thinly sliced red onion, mango chutney (optional)

1. Combine quinoa, lentils, water and ½ teaspoon salt in large saucepan. Bring to a boil over medium-high heat. Reduce heat to low; cover and simmer 15 minutes or until quinoa and lentils are tender. Drain any excess liquid. Place in large bowl.

2. Heat 1 tablespoon oil in large nonstick skillet over medium-high heat. Add onion and remaining 1 teaspoon salt; cook and stir 5 minutes or until onion is softened. Reduce heat to medium. Add peas; cook and stir 4 minutes. Add garlic and curry powder; cook and stir 30 seconds. Add to quinoa mixture with egg; mix well. Cool 15 minutes.

3. Scoop mixture by ½ cupfuls; shape into ½-inch-thick patties. If making ahead, place patties on baking sheet or large plate sprayed with nonstick cooking spray and refrigerate until ready to cook.

4. Heat 1 tablespoon oil in skillet over medium-high heat. Reduce heat to medium; gently place patties in skillet. Cook 4 to 5 minutes or until well browned on bottom. Add remaining 1 tablespoon oil to skillet, flip patties and continue cooking 4 to 5 minutes or until browned on other side.

5. Serve on buns with desired toppings.

SANDWICHES AND TOASTS

Vegetable-Bean Quesadillas

Makes 8 servings

1 tablespoon canola oil

1 cup sliced onion

1 can (15 ounces) black beans, rinsed and drained

1 cup sliced green bell pepper

1 cup sliced red bell pepper

½ teaspoon ground cumin

¼ teaspoon ground red pepper

8 (8-inch) whole grain tortillas

1 cup (4 ounces) shredded Cheddar cheese

Salsa (optional)

1. Heat oil in large nonstick skillet over medium-high heat. Add onion; cook and stir 2 minutes or until translucent. Add beans, bell peppers, cumin and ground red pepper; cook and stir 3 minutes or until bell peppers are crisp-tender.

2. Wipe out skillet with paper towels; heat skillet over medium heat. Spread about ⅓ cup vegetables on half of each tortilla; sprinkle with 2 tablespoons cheese. Fold tortilla over filling. Cook in batches until light brown on bottom. Turn and brown other side. Cut into wedges. Serve with salsa, if desired.

VEGAN: Replace Cheddar cheese with a vegan cheese alternative.

Tuscan Portobello Melt

Makes 2 servings

- 1 **portobello mushroom cap, thinly sliced**
- ½ **small red onion, thinly sliced**
- ½ **cup grape tomatoes**
- 1 **tablespoon olive oil**
- 1 **teaspoon balsamic vinegar**
- ⅛ **teaspoon salt**
- ⅛ **teaspoon dried thyme**
- ⅛ **teaspoon black pepper**
- 2 **tablespoons butter, softened, divided**
- 4 **slices sourdough bread**
- 2 **slices provolone cheese**
- 2 **teaspoons Dijon mustard**
- 2 **slices Monterey Jack cheese**

1. Preheat broiler. Combine mushroom, onion and tomatoes in small baking pan. Drizzle with oil and vinegar; sprinkle with salt, thyme and pepper. Toss to coat. Spread vegetables in single layer in pan.

2. Broil 6 minutes or until vegetables are softened and browned, stirring once.

3. Heat medium skillet over medium heat. Spread 1 tablespoon butter over one side of each bread slice. Place buttered side down in skillet; cook 2 minutes or until bread is toasted. Transfer bread to cutting board, toasted sides up.

4. Place provolone cheese on 2 bread slices; spread mustard over cheese. Top with vegetables, Monterey Jack cheese and remaining bread slices, toasted sides down. Spread remaining 1 tablespoon butter on outside of sandwiches. Cook in same skillet over medium heat 5 minutes or until bread is toasted and cheese is melted, turning once.

PICO DE GALLO

- **1 cup finely chopped tomatoes (about 2 small)**
- **½ teaspoon salt**
- **¼ cup chopped white onion**
- **2 tablespoons minced jalapeño pepper**
- **2 tablespoons chopped fresh cilantro**
- **1 teaspoon lime juice**

GUACAMOLE

- **2 large ripe avocados, halved and pitted**
- **¼ cup finely chopped red onion**
- **2 tablespoons chopped fresh cilantro**
- **2 teaspoons lime juice**
- **½ teaspoon salt**

WRAPS

- **4 whole wheat burrito-size tortillas (about 10 inches)**
- **2 cups fresh baby spinach leaves**
- **1 cup sliced mushrooms**
- **1 cup shredded Asiago cheese**
- **Salsa**

Spinach Veggie Wrap

Makes 4 servings

1. For pico de gallo, combine tomatoes and ½ teaspoon salt in fine-mesh strainer; set in bowl or sink to drain 15 minutes. Combine drained tomatoes, white onion, jalapeño, 2 tablespoons cilantro and 1 teaspoon lime juice in medium bowl; mix well.

2. For guacamole, scoop avocado into another medium bowl. Add red onion, 2 tablespoons cilantro, 2 teaspoons lime juice and ½ teaspoon salt; mash with fork to desired consistency.

3. For wraps, spread ¼ cup guacamole on each tortilla. Layer each with ½ cup spinach, ¼ cup mushrooms, ¼ cup cheese and ¼ cup pico de gallo. Roll up; serve with salsa.

VEGAN: Omit cheese or use a vegan cheese alternative.

MAKE AHEAD: Wraps make great packed lunches. Prepare the pico de gallo and guacamole ahead of time and store them in the refrigerator. Assemble the wraps as you need them and wrap them in plastic wrap to go.

SANDWICHES AND TOASTS

Mediterranean Vegetable Sandwich

Makes 4 sandwiches

½ **cup plain hummus**

½ **jalapeño pepper, seeded and minced**

¼ **cup minced fresh cilantro**

8 **slices whole wheat bread**

4 **leaves lettuce (leaf or Bibb lettuce)**

2 **tomatoes, thinly sliced**

½ **cucumber, thinly sliced**

½ **red onion, thinly sliced**

½ **cup thinly sliced peppadew peppers or sweet Italian peppers**

4 **tablespoons crumbled feta cheese**

1. Combine hummus, jalapeño and cilantro in small bowl; mix well.

2. Spread about 1 tablespoon hummus mixture on one side of each bread slice. Layer half of bread slices with lettuce, tomatoes, cucumber, onion, peppadew peppers and feta; top with remaining bread slices. Cut sandwiches in half.

VEGAN: Omit feta cheese.

Black Bean Burgers with Spicy Mayo

Makes 4 servings

5 whole wheat hamburger buns (1½ to 2 ounces each), split, divided

1 can (15 ounces) black beans, rinsed and well drained

½ cup (2 ounces) Cheddar cheese or Mexican blend cheese

2 egg whites

2 green onions, sliced

1 teaspoon chili powder

1 teaspoon dried oregano

½ teaspoon garlic salt

1 tablespoon canola oil

2 tablespoons mayonnaise

¾ teaspoon chipotle hot pepper sauce

Lettuce and tomato slices

1. Tear 1 hamburger bun into pieces; place in bowl of food processor. Process until coarse crumbs form. Transfer to medium bowl.

2. Add beans, cheese, egg whites, green onions, chili powder, oregano and garlic salt to food processor. Process to a thick paste, scraping down sides of bowl once. Add mixture to bread crumbs in bowl; mix well.

3. Heat oil in large nonstick skillet over medium heat. Scoop mixture into 4 mounds in skillet by by ½ cupfuls; press down to form 4-inch patties. Cook 4 minutes per side or until browned. Lightly toast remaining hamburger buns, if desired.

4. Combine mayonnaise and hot pepper sauce in small bowl. Serve patties in buns with mayonnaise mixture, lettuce and tomato.

Avocado Toast

Makes 2 servings

½ cup thawed frozen peas

2 teaspoons lemon juice

1 teaspoon minced fresh tarragon

¼ teaspoon plus ⅛ teaspoon salt, divided

⅛ teaspoon black pepper

1 teaspoon olive oil

1 tablespoon pepitas (raw pumpkin seeds)

4 slices hearty whole grain bread, toasted

1 avocado

1. Combine peas, lemon juice, tarragon, ¼ teaspoon salt and pepper in small food processor; pulse until blended but still chunky. Or combine all ingredients in small bowl and mash with fork to desired consistency.

2. Heat oil in small saucepan over medium heat. Add pepitas; cook and stir 1 to 2 minutes or until toasted. Transfer to small bowl; stir in remaining ⅛ teaspoon salt.

3. Spread about 1 tablespoon pea mixture over each slice of bread. If making one serving, place the remaining pea mixture in a jar or container and store in the refrigerator for a day or two.

4. Cut avocado in half lengthwise around pit. If making one serving, wrap the half with the pit in plastic wrap and store in the refrigerator for a day. Cut the avocado into slices in the shell; use a spoon to scoop the slices out of the shell. Arrange avocado slices on the toast; top with toasted pepitas.

1 can (15 ounces)
chickpeas, rinsed
and drained

¼ cup chopped fresh
parsley

¼ cup soft cream cheese

1 tablespoon chopped
fresh dill *or*
1 teaspoon dried
dill weed

1 tablespoon milk

⅛ teaspoon black
pepper

8 very thin slices wheat
bread, toasted

¼ cup (1 ounce)
shredded mozzarella
cheese

Chickpea Toasts

Makes 4 servings

1. Preheat broiler. Place beans, parsley, cream cheese, dill, milk and pepper in food processor. Pulse until almost smooth.

2. Spread bean mixture on toast. Sprinkle with cheese. Place on ungreased baking sheet. Broil 4 inches from heat source 2 to 3 minutes or until cheese is melted and sandwiches are heated through.

MAKE AHEAD: Prepare the chickpea mixture ahead of time and store it in the refrigerator until needed.

BALSAMIC VINAIGRETTE

- 6 **tablespoons extra virgin olive oil**
- 3 **tablespoons balsamic vinegar**
- 1 **clove garlic, minced**
- 1 **teaspoon honey**
- 1 **teaspoon Dijon mustard**
- ½ **teaspoon dried oregano**
- ½ **teaspoon salt**
- ⅛ **teaspoon black pepper**

SANDWICHES

- 1 **baguette, ends trimmed, cut into 4 equal pieces (4 ounces each) and split**
- 1 **cup loosely packed baby arugula**
- 3 **medium tomatoes, sliced ¼ inch thick**
- 1 **cup roasted red peppers, patted dry and thinly sliced**
- 1 **package (8 ounces) presliced fresh mozzarella (12 slices)**
- 12 **fresh basil leaves**

Tomato Mozzarella Sandwich

Makes 4 servings

1. For vinaigrette, whisk oil, vinegar, garlic, honey, mustard, oregano, salt and pepper in small bowl until well blended.

2. For each sandwich, drizzle 1 tablespoon vinaigrette over bottom half of bread. Layer with arugula, tomato slices, roasted peppers, cheese, additional arugula and basil. Drizzle with 1 tablespoon dressing; replace top half of bread.

MAKE AHEAD: Make the vinaigrette ahead of time and store it in the refrigerator. Assemble individual sandwiches as needed.

Southwestern Flatbread with Black Beans and Corn

Makes 4 servings

- 2 **oval flatbreads (11×7 inches)**
- ¼ **cup prepared green chile enchilada sauce**
- 2 **cups (8 ounces) shredded Monterey Jack cheese**
- 1 **can (15 ounces) black beans, rinsed and drained**
- 1 **cup frozen corn, thawed**
- ½ **cup finely chopped red onion**
- 1 **teaspoon olive oil**
- ½ **teaspoon kosher salt**
- 1 **avocado, diced**
- 2 **tablespoons fresh chopped cilantro**
- **Lime wedges (optional)**

1. Preheat oven to 425°F. Place wire rack on large baking sheet; place flatbreads on rack.

2. Spread enchilada sauce over flatbreads; sprinkle with cheese. Combine beans, corn, onion, oil and salt in medium bowl. Layer mixture on top of cheese. Bake 12 minutes or until flatbreads are golden and crisp and cheese is melted.

3. Arrange avocado on flatbreads; sprinkle with cilantro. Cut into pieces to serve. Serve with lime wedges, if desired.

Chickpea, Roasted Pepper and Olive Toasts

Makes 24 toasts

2 cloves garlic, peeled

1 can (15 ounces) chickpeas, rinsed and drained

1 cup chopped drained roasted red peppers

¼ cup olive oil

Salt and black pepper

½ cup drained pitted black olives

½ cup drained pimiento-stuffed green olives

24 (½-inch) toasted French bread slices

1. Turn on food processor; drop garlic through feed tube. Add chickpeas and roasted peppers; process until paste forms. With motor running, add oil in thin steady stream; process until smooth. Transfer chickpea mixture to medium bowl; season with salt and black pepper. Cover and let stand 30 minutes.

2. Place black and green olives in clean food processor. Pulse until olives are coarsely chopped.

3. Spread 2 tablespoons chickpea mixture on each bread slice. Spoon 1 tablespoon olive mixture in center of chickpea mixture. Serve at room temperature.

NOTE: Leftover chickpea mixture makes a great dip for fresh vegetables.

MAKE-AHEAD: Chickpea and olive mixtures can both be prepared up to 2 days in advance. Store separately in airtight containers in the refrigerator.

Zoodles in Tomato Sauce

Makes 4 servings

1. Heat 2 teaspoons oil in medium saucepan over medium heat. Add garlic; cook 1 minute or until fragrant but not browned. Stir in tomato paste; cook 30 seconds, stirring constantly. Add tomatoes with juice, oregano and salt; break up tomatoes with wooden spoon. Bring to a simmer. Reduce heat; cook 30 minutes or until thickened.

2. Meanwhile, spiral zucchini with fine spiral blade. Heat remaining 1 teaspoon oil in large skillet over medium-high heat. Add zucchini; cook 4 to 5 minutes or until tender, stirring frequently. Transfer to serving plates; top with tomato sauce and Parmesan cheese, if desired.

NOTE: If you don't have a spiralizer, buy packaged zucchini noodles from the produce section of large supermarkets. Or cut the zucchini into ribbons with a mandoline, a julienne peeler or sharp knife.

VEGAN: Omit cheese.

3 teaspoons olive oil, divided

2 cloves garlic

1 tablespoon tomato paste

1 can (28 ounces) whole tomatoes, undrained

1 teaspoon dried oregano

½ teaspoon salt

2 large zucchini (about 16 ounces each), ends trimmed, cut into 3-inch pieces

¼ cup shredded Parmesan cheese

Jalapeño Beans

Makes 4 to 6 servings

1 tablespoon vegetable oil

1 small onion, finely chopped

1 teaspoon ground cumin

1 teaspoon garlic powder

½ teaspoon smoked paprika

¼ teaspoon ground red pepper

3 tablespoons chopped pickled jalapeño peppers

2 cans (15 ounces each) chili beans (made with pinto beans)

⅓ cup dark lager beer

1 tablespoon white vinegar

1 teaspoon sugar

½ teaspoon hot pepper sauce

Salt and black pepper

1. Heat oil in medium saucepan over medium-high heat. Add onion; cook and stir 2 minutes or until translucent. Add cumin, garlic powder, paprika and red pepper; cook and stir 1 minute. Add pickled jalapeños; cook and stir 30 seconds.

2. Stir in beans, beer, vinegar, sugar and hot pepper sauce; bring to a boil. Reduce heat to medium-low; cook 15 minutes, stirring occasionally. Season with salt and black pepper. Beans will thicken upon standing.

NF Q EF V DF MA

Spinach and Mushroom Enchiladas

Makes 4 servings

2 packages (10 ounces each) frozen chopped spinach, thawed and squeezed dry

1½ cups sliced mushrooms

1 can (15 ounces) pinto beans, rinsed and drained

3 teaspoons chili powder, divided

½ teaspoon salt

¼ teaspoon red pepper flakes

1 can (8 ounces) tomato sauce

2 tablespoons water

½ teaspoon hot pepper sauce

8 (8-inch) corn tortillas

1 cup (4 ounces) shredded Monterey Jack cheese

Optional garnishes: shredded lettuce, chopped tomatoes, sour cream and/ or chopped fresh cilantro

1. Combine spinach, mushrooms, beans, 2 teaspoons chili powder, salt and red pepper flakes in large skillet; cook and stir over medium heat 5 minutes. Combine tomato sauce, water, remaining 1 teaspoon chili powder and hot pepper sauce in medium skillet.

2. Dip each tortilla into tomato sauce mixture. Spoon filling evenly onto center of tortillas; roll up and place seam side down in 11×8-inch microwavable dish. Secure rolls with toothpicks, if necessary. Spread remaining tomato sauce mixture over enchiladas.

3. Cover with vented plastic wrap. Microwave on MEDIUM (50%) 10 minutes or until heated through. Sprinkle with cheese. Microwave on MEDIUM 3 minutes or until cheese is melted. Serve with desired toppings. Remove toothpicks before serving.

Sweet Potato and Apple Casserole

Makes 8 servings

- 1 **cup all-purpose flour**
- ¾ **cup (1½ sticks) butter, melted, divided**
- ½ **cup packed brown sugar**
- 1 **teaspoon salt, divided**
- ½ **teaspoon ground cinnamon**
- ¼ **teaspoon ground nutmeg or mace**
- ¼ **teaspoon ground cardamom**
- 2 **pounds sweet potatoes, peeled, halved lengthwise and thinly sliced**
- 2 **Granny Smith apples, peeled, cored, halved lengthwise and thinly sliced**

1. Preheat oven to 375°F. Spray 2-quart baking dish with nonstick cooking spray.

2. Combine flour, ½ cup butter, brown sugar, ½ teaspoon salt, cinnamon, nutmeg and cardamom in medium bowl until well blended.

3. Arrange sweet potatoes and apples in prepared baking dish. Drizzle with remaining ¼ cup butter; sprinkle with remaining ½ teaspoon with salt.

4. Crumble topping over sweet potatoes and apples. Bake 35 to 40 minutes or until topping is brown and potatoes and apples are tender.

Pesto Rice and Beans

Makes 8 servings

1 can (15 ounces) Great Northern beans, rinsed and drained

1 can (about 14 ounces) vegetable broth

¾ cup uncooked long-grain white rice

1½ cups frozen cut green beans, thawed and drained

½ cup prepared pesto

Grated Parmesan cheese (optional)

SLOW COOKER DIRECTIONS

1. Combine Great Northern beans, broth and rice in slow cooker. Cover; cook on LOW 2 hours.

2. Stir in green beans; cover and cook on LOW 1 hour or until rice and beans are tender.

3. Turn off slow cooker and remove insert to heatproof surface. Stir in pesto and Parmesan cheese, if desired. Let stand, covered, 5 minutes or until cheese is melted. Serve immediately.

Roasted Balsamic Asparagus

Makes 6 servings

- 1 **pound fresh asparagus**
- 1 **tablespoon olive oil**
- ½ **teaspoon salt**
- ¼ **teaspoon black pepper**
- 1 **tablespoon balsamic glaze***
- ¼ **cup finely shredded or grated Parmesan cheese**

*Balsamic glaze can be found in the condiment section of the supermarket or can be prepared by simmering 2 tablespoons balsamic vinegar in small saucepan until reduced by about half.

1. Preheat oven to 375°F.

2. Arrange asparagus in single layer in shallow 11×7-inch baking dish. Drizzle asparagus with oil; gently roll to coat evenly. Sprinkle with salt and pepper.

3. Bake 14 to 16 minutes or until crisp-tender. Drizzle balsamic glaze over asparagus; roll again with tongs to coat. Top with cheese.

VEGAN: Omit cheese.

Red Beans and Rice with Pickled Carrots and Cucumbers

Makes 6 servings

Pickled Carrots
and Cucumbers
(page 153)

1 pound dried red
kidney beans

1 tablespoon plus
1 teaspoon salt,
divided

2 tablespoons olive oil

2 onions, chopped

3 stalks celery, chopped

1 green bell pepper,
chopped

4 cloves garlic, minced

4 cups vegetable broth

1 teaspoon liquid smoke

1 bay leaf

2 teaspoons Italian
seasoning

½ teaspoon black
pepper

¼ teaspoon ground
red pepper

½ cup water

Hot cooked brown rice

Sliced avocado

Hot pepper sauce

1. Prepare pickled carrots and cucumbers. Place beans in large bowl. Cover with water and stir in 1 tablespoon salt. Soak 8 hours or overnight. Drain.

2. Heat oil in large saucepan over medium-high heat. Add onions; cook and stir 5 minutes. Season with remaining 1 teaspoon salt. Add celery, bell pepper and garlic; cook and stir 5 minutes or until vegetables are tender.

3. Add beans, broth, liquid smoke, bay leaf, Italian seasoning, black pepper and red pepper; bring to a boil. Reduce heat; simmer, partially covered, 45 minutes. Remove 2 cups bean mixture to medium bowl; let stand 15 minutes to cool slightly. Place in blender or food processor and add ½ cup water; blend until smooth. Stir into beans; continue to cook until beans are tender. Taste and season with additional salt, if desired. Remove and discard bay leaf. Serve with pickled vegetables, rice, avocado and hot pepper sauce.

NF GF EF V DF MA

NF Q GF EF V DF MA

Pickled Carrots and Cucumbers

2 carrots

1 cucumber

¼ cup water

2 tablespoons sugar

1 tablespoon salt

1 teaspoon peppercorns

2 cloves garlic, smashed

¼ teaspoon dried dill

2 bay leaves

1½ cups white vinegar

1. Thinly slice carrots into coins. Very thinly slice cucumber (⅟₁₆-inch slices) with a mandoline if you have one or a sharp knife. Place carrots and cucumbers in 1-quart jar.

2. Combine water, sugar, salt, peppercorns, garlic, dill and bay leaves in small saucepan. Cook over medium heat until salt and sugar are dissolved. Pour over vegetables in jar. Add enough vinegar to cover. Seal jar and refrigerate at least 2 hours. Can be made a few days in advance.

Fried Green Tomato Parmesan

Makes 4 servings

- 2 cans (15 ounces each) tomato sauce
- 4 green tomatoes, thickly sliced into 3 slices each
- ½ teaspoon salt, divided
- Black pepper
- ½ cup all-purpose flour
- 1 teaspoon Italian seasoning
- 2 eggs
- 2 tablespoons water
- 1½ cups panko bread crumbs
- 4 tablespoons olive oil, divided
- ½ cup shredded Parmesan cheese
- Shredded fresh basil
- Hot cooked spaghetti (optional)

1. Preheat oven to 350°F. Spread 1 cup tomato sauce in 9-inch square baking dish. Sprinkle one side of tomatoes with ¼ teaspoon salt; season lightly with pepper.

2. Combine flour, Italian seasoning and remaining ¼ teaspoon salt in shallow bowl. Whisk eggs and water in another shallow bowl. Place panko in third shallow bowl. Coat tomatoes with flour mixture. Dip in egg mixture, letting excess drip back into bowl. Dredge in panko, pressing onto all sides.

3. Heat 2 tablespoons oil in large skillet over medium-high heat. Add half of tomatoes; cook 3 minutes per side or until panko is golden brown. Arrange tomatoes in single layer in sauce in baking dish. Sprinkle 1 teaspoon cheese on each tomato; spread some sauce over tomatoes. Heat remaining 2 tablespoons oil in same skillet; cook remaining tomatoes 3 minutes per side until coating is golden brown. Stagger tomatoes in second layer over tomatoes in baking dish. Top each tomato with 1 teaspoon cheese and spread 1 cup sauce over top. Sprinkle with remaining cheese.

4. Bake 20 minutes or until cheese is melted and sauce is heated through. Heat remaining tomato sauce. Serve tomatoes with basil, sauce and spaghetti, if desired.

NF

VEGETABLES AND LEGUMES

Smashed Potatoes

Makes 4 servings

- 4 **medium russet potatoes (about 1½ pounds), peeled and cut into ¼-inch cubes**
- ⅓ **cup milk**
- 2 **tablespoons sour cream**
- 1 **tablespoon minced onion**
- ½ **teaspoon salt**
- ¼ **teaspoon black pepper**
- ⅛ **teaspoon garlic powder (optional)**

  Chopped fresh chives (optional)

1. Bring large saucepan of lightly salted water to a boil. Add potatoes; cook 15 to 20 minutes or until fork-tender. Drain and return to saucepan.

2. Slightly mash potatoes. Stir in milk, sour cream, minced onion, salt, pepper and garlic powder, if desired. Mash until desired texture is reached, leaving potatoes chunky. Cook 5 minutes over low heat until heated through, stirring occasionally. Top with chives, if desired.

VEGETABLES AND LEGUMES

Garlic-Cilantro Green Beans

Makes 4 to 6 servings

1½ **pounds green beans, ends trimmed**

3 **tablespoons olive oil**

1 **red bell pepper, cut into thin strips**

½ **sweet onion, halved and thinly sliced**

2 **teaspoons minced garlic**

1 **teaspoon salt**

2 **tablespoons chopped fresh cilantro**

Black pepper

1. Bring large saucepan of salted water to a boil over medium-high heat. Add beans; cook 6 minutes or until tender. Drain and return to saucepan.

2. Meanwhile, heat oil in large skillet over medium-high heat. Add bell pepper and onion; cook and stir 3 minutes or until vegetables are tender but not browned. Add garlic; cook and stir 30 seconds. Add beans and salt; cook and stir 2 minutes or until heated through and beans are coated with oil. Stir in cilantro; season with black pepper. Serve immediately.

NF Q GF EF V DF

Layered Mexican-Style Casserole

Makes 6 servings

- 2 cans (15 ounces each) hominy, drained*
- 1 can (15 ounces) black beans, rinsed and drained
- 1 can (about 14 ounces) diced tomatoes with garlic, basil and oregano
- 1 cup thick and chunky salsa
- 1 can (6 ounces) tomato paste
- ½ teaspoon ground cumin
- ¼ teaspoon salt
- 3 (9-inch) flour tortillas
- 2 cups (8 ounces) shredded Monterey Jack cheese
- ¼ cup sliced black olives

Hominy is corn that has been treated to remove the germ and hull. It can be found with the canned vegetables or beans in most supermarkets.

SLOW COOKER DIRECTIONS

1. Prepare foil handles (see below). Spray inside of slow cooker with nonstick cooking spray.

2. Combine hominy, beans, tomatoes, salsa, tomato paste, cumin and salt in large bowl.

3. Press 1 tortilla in bottom of slow cooker. (Edges of tortilla may turn up slightly.) Top with one third of hominy mixture and one third of cheese. Repeat layers. Press remaining tortilla on top. Top with remaining hominy mixture. Set aside remaining cheese.

4. Cover; cook on LOW 6 to 8 hours. Sprinkle with remaining cheese and olives. Cover; let stand 5 minutes. Pull out tortilla stack with foil handles. Cut into wedges.

FOIL HANDLES: Tear off three (18×2-inch) strips of heavy-duty foil or use regular foil folded to double thickness. Crisscross foil strips in spoke design and place into slow cooker to make removing the tortilla stack easier.

GLUTEN-FREE: Use corn tortillas instead of flour tortillas.

Mexican-Style Corn on the Cob

Makes 4 servings

¼ cup mayonnaise

1 teaspoon chili powder

1 teaspoon grated lime peel

4 ears corn, shucked

¼ cup grated cotija or Parmesan cheese

1. Prepare grill for direct cooking. Combine mayonnaise, chili powder and lime peel in small bowl.

2. Grill corn over medium-high heat 4 to 6 minutes or until lightly charred, turning occasionally. Immediately spread mayonnaise mixture over corn. Sprinkle with cheese.

NOTE: Corn can be broiled or cooked in a dry cast iron skillet instead of grilling. Or remove the kernels from the cobs and cook 2 minutes in lightly salted boiling water. Drain well, place in a medium bowl and stir in the remaining ingredients.

NF Q GF EF

Channa Chat (Indian-Spiced Snack Mix)

Makes 6 to 8 servings

- 2 teaspoons canola oil
- 1 medium onion, finely chopped, divided
- 2 cloves garlic, minced
- 2 cans (15 ounces each) chickpeas, rinsed and drained
- ¼ cup vegetable broth or water
- 2 teaspoons tomato paste
- ¼ teaspoon ground cinnamon
- ¼ teaspoon ground cumin
- ¼ teaspoon black pepper
- 1 bay leaf
- ½ cup balsamic vinegar
- 1 tablespoon packed brown sugar
- 1 plum tomato, chopped
- ½ jalapeño pepper, minced *or* ¼ teaspoon ground red pepper (optional)
- ½ cup crisp rice cereal
- 3 tablespoons chopped fresh cilantro (optional)

SLOW COOKER DIRECTIONS

1. Heat oil in small skillet over medium heat. Add half of onion and garlic; cook and stir 2 minutes or until softened. Transfer to slow cooker. Stir in chickpeas, broth, tomato paste, cinnamon, cumin, black pepper and bay leaf.

2. Cover; cook on LOW 6 hours or on HIGH 3 hours. Remove and discard bay leaf.

3. Transfer chickpeas to large shallow bowl with slotted spoon; let cool 15 minutes. Meanwhile, combine balsamic vinegar and brown sugar in small saucepan. Cook over medium-low heat until mixture becomes syrupy.

4. Toss chickpeas with tomato, remaining onion and jalapeño, if desired. Fold in rice cereal and drizzle with balsamic syrup. Garnish with cilantro.

NF GF EF V DF MA

SWEETS AND TREATS

Lemon Squares

Makes 2 to 3 dozen bars

1. Beat butter, ½ cup granulated sugar and salt in large bowl with electric mixer on medium speed until light and fluffy. Add 2 cups flour; mix on low speed just until blended.

2. Press dough into 13×9-inch baking pan, building edges up ½ inch on all sides. Refrigerate 20 minutes or until slightly firm.

3. Preheat oven to 350°F. Bake 15 to 20 minutes or until very lightly browned. Cool on wire rack.

4. Whisk 3 cups granulated sugar, 1 cup flour, eggs and egg yolks, lemon juice, lemon peel and baking powder in large bowl until well blended. Pour over crust.

5. Bake 30 to 35 minutes until filling is set. Cool completely in pan on wire rack. Sprinkle with powdered sugar; cut into squares. Store leftovers in refrigerator.

CRUST

- 1 cup (2 sticks) butter, softened
- ½ cup granulated sugar
- ½ teaspoon salt
- 2 cups all-purpose flour

FILLING

- 3 cups granulated sugar
- 1 cup all-purpose flour
- 4 eggs plus 2 egg yolks, at room temperature
- ⅔ cup fresh lemon juice
- 2 tablespoons grated lemon peel
- ½ teaspoon baking powder

  Powdered sugar

SWEETS AND TREATS

Cinnamon Apples

Makes 4 servings

¼ cup (½ stick) butter

3 tart red apples such as Gala, Fuji or Honeycrisp (about 1½ pounds total), peeled and cut into ½-inch wedges

¼ cup packed brown sugar

1 teaspoon ground cinnamon

⅛ teaspoon ground nutmeg

⅛ teaspoon salt

1 tablespoon cornstarch

1. Melt butter in large skillet over medium-high heat. Add apples; cook about 8 minutes or until apples are tender, stirring occasionally.

2. Add brown sugar, cinnamon, nutmeg and salt; cook and stir 1 minute or until glazed. Reduce heat to medium-low; stir in cornstarch until well blended.

3. Remove from heat; let stand 5 minutes for glaze to thicken. Stir again; serve immediately.

Plum Rhubarb Crumble

Makes 6 to 8 servings

1½ **pounds plums, pitted and cut into wedges (4 cups)**

1½ **pounds rhubarb, cut into ½-inch pieces (5 cups)**

1 **cup granulated sugar**

1 **teaspoon finely grated fresh ginger**

¼ **teaspoon ground nutmeg**

3 **tablespoons cornstarch**

¾ **cup old-fashioned oats**

½ **cup all-purpose flour**

½ **cup packed brown sugar or palm sugar**

½ **cup sliced almonds, toasted***

¼ **teaspoon salt**

½ **cup (1 stick) cold butter, cut into small pieces**

To toast almonds, spread in single layer on ungreased baking sheet. Bake in preheated 350°F oven 5 minutes or until golden brown, stirring frequently.

1. Combine plums, rhubarb, granulated sugar, ginger and nutmeg in large bowl; toss to coat. Cover and let stand at room temperature 2 hours.

2. Preheat oven to 375°F. Spray 9-inch round or square baking dish with nonstick cooking spray. Line baking sheet with foil.

3. Pour juices from fruit into small saucepan; bring to a boil over medium-high heat. Cook about 12 minutes or until reduced to syrupy consistency, stirring occasionally. Stir in cornstarch until well blended. Stir mixture into bowl with fruit; pour into prepared baking dish.

4. Combine oats, flour, brown sugar, almonds and salt in medium bowl; mix well. Add butter; mix with fingertips until butter is evenly distributed and mixture is clumpy. Sprinkle evenly over fruit mixture. Place baking dish on prepared baking sheet.

5. Bake about 50 minutes or until filling is bubbly and topping is golden brown. Cool 1 hour before serving.

Cinnamon-Wheat Brownies

Makes 16 brownies

2 ounces unsweetened chocolate

½ cup (1 stick) butter, softened

1 cup packed dark brown sugar

2 eggs

1 teaspoon ground cinnamon

1 teaspoon vanilla

¼ teaspoon baking powder

¼ teaspoon ground ginger

⅛ teaspoon ground cloves

½ cup whole wheat flour

1 cup coarsely chopped walnuts

1. Preheat oven to 350°F. Butter 8-inch square baking pan. Melt chocolate in top of double boiler over simmering water. Cool.

2. Beat butter, brown sugar, eggs and melted chocolate in large bowl with electric mixer at medium speed until light and smooth. Blend in cinnamon, vanilla, baking powder, ginger and cloves. Stir in flour and walnuts until well blended. Spread batter evenly in prepared pan.

3. Bake 25 minutes or until top feels firm and dry. Cool completely in pan on wire rack. Cut into 2-inch squares.

Warm Apple Crostata

Makes 4 tarts (4 to 8 servings)

1¾ cups all-purpose flour

⅓ cup granulated sugar

½ teaspoon plus
⅛ teaspoon salt,
divided

¾ cup (1½ sticks) cold
butter, cut into small
pieces

3 tablespoons ice water

2 teaspoons vanilla

8 Pink Lady or
Honeycrisp apples
(about 1½ pounds),
peeled and cut into
¼-inch slices

¼ cup packed brown
sugar or palm sugar

1 tablespoon lemon
juice

1 teaspoon ground
cinnamon

⅛ teaspoon ground
nutmeg

4 teaspoons butter, cut
into very small pieces

1 egg, beaten

1 to 2 teaspoons coarse
sugar

Vanilla ice cream

Caramel sauce or
ice cream topping

1. Combine flour, ⅓ cup granulated sugar and ½ teaspoon salt in food processor; process 5 seconds. Add ¾ cup butter; process about 10 seconds or until mixture resembles coarse crumbs.

2. Combine ice water and vanilla in small bowl. With motor running, pour mixture through feed tube; process 12 seconds or until dough begins to come together. Shape dough into a disc; wrap in plastic wrap and refrigerate 30 minutes.

3. Meanwhile, combine apples, brown sugar, lemon juice, cinnamon, nutmeg and remaining ⅛ teaspoon salt in large bowl; toss to coat. Preheat oven to 400°F.

4. Line two baking sheets with parchment paper. Cut dough into 4 pieces; roll out each piece into 7-inch circle on floured surface. Place circles on prepared baking sheets; mound apples in center of dough circles (about 1 cup apples for each crostata). Fold or roll up edges of dough towards center to create rim of crostata. Dot apples with remaining 4 teaspoons butter. Brush dough with egg; sprinkle dough and apples with coarse sugar.

5. Bake about 20 minutes or until apples are tender and crust is golden brown. Serve warm topped with ice cream and caramel sauce.

SWEETS AND TREATS

Gingery Oat and Molasses Cookies

Makes about 4 dozen cookies

1 cup all-purpose flour

¾ cup whole wheat flour

½ cup old-fashioned oats

1½ teaspoons baking powder

1½ teaspoons ground ginger

1 teaspoon baking soda

½ teaspoon ground cinnamon

¼ teaspoon salt

¾ cup sugar

½ cup (1 stick) butter, softened

1 egg

¼ cup molasses

¼ teaspoon vanilla

1 cup chopped crystallized ginger

½ cup chopped walnuts

1. Combine all-purpose flour, whole wheat flour, oats, baking powder, ground ginger, baking soda, cinnamon and salt in medium bowl; mix well. Beat sugar and butter in large bowl with electric mixer on high speed until light and fluffy. Beat in egg, molasses and vanilla. Gradually beat in flour mixture. Stir in crystallized ginger and walnuts.

2. Shape dough into 2 (8- to 10-inch) logs. Wrap in plastic wrap; refrigerate 1 to 3 hours.

3. Preheat oven to 350°F. Line baking sheets with parchment paper. Cut logs into ⅓-inch slices; place 1½ inches apart on prepared baking sheets.

4. Bake 12 to 14 minutes or until set. Cool on cookie sheets 5 minutes. Remove to wire racks; cool completely.

Vegan Chocolate Cake

Makes 12 to 16 servings

CAKE

- 6 **tablespoons boiling water**
- 2 **tablespoons ground flaxseed**
- 2 **cups granulated sugar**
- 2 **cups all-purpose flour**
- 1 **cup unsweetened cocoa powder**
- 1 **tablespoon instant espresso powder***
- 2 **teaspoons baking soda**
- 1½ **teaspoons baking powder**
- 1½ **teaspoons salt**
- ¾ **cup plain unsweetened almond milk**
- ½ **cup vegetable oil**
- 1 **tablespoon apple cider vinegar**
- 2 **teaspoons vanilla**
- 1 **cup hot water***

FROSTING

- 1 **package (12 ounces) vegan chocolate chips**
- ¼ **teaspoon salt**
- 1 **can (about 13 ounces) full-fat coconut milk**
- 2 **cups powdered sugar**

Or substitute 1 cup hot strong brewed coffee.

1. Preheat oven to 350°F. Line 13×9-inch baking pan with parchment paper or spray with nonstick cooking spray. Combine boiling water and flaxseed in small bowl; cool completely.

2. Whisk granulated sugar, flour, cocoa, espresso powder, baking soda, baking powder and 1½ teaspoons salt in large bowl. Make well in center. Pour almond milk, oil, vinegar, vanilla and flaxseed mixture into well; whisk gently to blend wet ingredients. Whisk into dry ingredients until moistened. Add hot water; whisk until well blended. Pour into prepared pan; smooth top.

3. Bake 30 to 35 minutes or until top appears dry and toothpick inserted into center comes out clean. Cool completely in pan on wire rack.

4. For frosting, place chocolate chips and ¼ teaspoon salt in bowl of electric stand mixer. Bring coconut milk to a simmer in small saucepan over medium heat, whisking frequently to blend. Pour 1 cup coconut milk over chips; swirl to coat. Let stand 5 minutes; whisk until smooth. Cool to room temperature.** Add powdered sugar; beat on low speed until blended. Increase speed to medium-high; beat 1 to 2 minutes or until frosting is fluffy and smooth. If frosting is too thick, add remaining coconut milk by teaspoonfuls until desired consistency is reached.

**To frost cake with ganache instead of frosting, spread cooled mixture over top of cake (skip the powdered sugar). For firm ganache, refrigerate until set.

NOTE: This cake keeps very well at room temperature (frosted or unfrosted) for a few days—just cover it tightly with plastic wrap.

NF EF V DF MA

SWEETS AND TREATS

Swedish Apple Pie

Makes 1 (9-inch) pie

4 Granny Smith apples, peeled, cored and sliced

1 cup plus 1 tablespoon sugar, divided

1 tablespoon ground cinnamon

¾ cup (1½ sticks) butter, melted

1 cup all-purpose flour

1 egg

½ cup chopped nuts

1. Preheat oven to 350°F.

2. Spread apples in 9-inch deep-dish pie plate or 9-inch square baking dish. Combine 1 tablespoon sugar and cinnamon in small bowl; sprinkle over apples and drizzle with butter.

3. Combine remaining 1 cup sugar, flour, egg and nuts in medium bowl; mix well. (Mixture will be thick.) Spread batter over apples.

4. Bake 50 to 55 minutes or until top is golden brown.

Q

Berry Shortcake Trifles

Makes 4 (1-pint) jars

LEMON CURD

- 1 **cup granulated sugar**
- ½ **cup (1 stick) butter**
- ⅔ **cup fresh lemon juice**
- 1 **tablespoon grated lemon peel**
- ¼ **teaspoon salt**
- 4 **eggs, beaten**

BERRIES

- 8 **ounces fresh strawberries, stemmed and diced**
- 8 **ounces fresh blueberries**
- ⅓ **cup granulated sugar**

WHIPPED CREAM

- 4 **ounces cream cheese, softened**
- 6 **tablespoons powdered sugar, divided**
- 1 **cup whipping cream, divided**
- ¼ **teaspoon vanilla**
- 1 **prepared pound cake (about 14 ounces), cut into ½-inch cubes**

1. Combine 1 cup granulated sugar, butter, lemon juice, lemon peel and salt in medium saucepan over medium heat, stirring until butter is melted and sugar is dissolved. Gradually whisk in eggs in thin steady stream. Cook over medium-low heat 5 minutes or until thickened to the consistency of pudding, whisking constantly. Strain through fine-mesh sieve into medium bowl. Press plastic wrap onto surface; refrigerate at least 2 hours or until cold.

2. Meanwhile, combine strawberries, blueberries and ⅓ cup granulated sugar in medium bowl. Cover and refrigerate at least 2 hours.

3. Beat cream cheese, 3 tablespoons powdered sugar, 2 tablespoons whipping cream and vanilla in large bowl with electric mixer on medium speed 3 minutes or until smooth. In separate bowl, beat remaining whipping cream and remaining 3 tablespoons powdered sugar to stiff peaks with electric mixer on high speed. Fold into cream cheese mixture until well blended.

4. Drain berries, reserving juice. Place ½ cup pound cake cubes in each of four wide-mouth 1-pint jars. Sprinkle cake cubes in each jar with 3 teaspoons reserved juice. Top with scant ¼ cup whipped cream, 2 tablespoons lemon curd and 1 tablespoon berries. Repeat layers. Refrigerate overnight.

Warm Mixed Berry Pie

Makes 8 servings

1¼ cups all-purpose flour

½ teaspoon salt

6 tablespoons cold butter, cubed

3 to 4 tablespoons ice water

½ teaspoon cider vinegar

2 packages (12 ounces each) frozen mixed berries

⅓ cup sugar

3 tablespoons cornstarch

2 teaspoons grated orange peel

¼ teaspoon ground ginger

1. Combine flour and salt in medium bowl. Cut in butter with pastry blender or two knives until mixture resembles coarse crumbs.

2. Combine 3 tablespoons water and vinegar in small bowl. Add to flour mixture; mix with fork until dough forms, adding additional water as needed. Turn out dough onto work surface; shape into a disc. Wrap in plastic wrap and refrigerate at least 30 minutes.

3. Preheat oven to 350°F. Roll out dough on lightly floured surface into 12-inch circle.

4. Combine berries, sugar, cornstarch, orange peel and ginger in large bowl; toss to coat. Spoon evenly into large cast iron skillet. Place crust over skillet; flute edge as desired. Cut slits in pie crust to allow steam to escape.

5. Bake 1 hour or until crust is golden brown. Let stand 1 hour before slicing and serving.

INDEX

ICON INDEX

 DAIRY-FREE

 EGG-FREE

GF GLUTEN-FREE

MA MAKE-AHEAD

NF NUT-FREE

QUICK PREP

V **VEGAN**

METRIC CONVERSION CHART

VOLUME MEASUREMENTS (dry)

1/8 teaspoon = 0.5 mL
1/4 teaspoon = 1 mL
1/2 teaspoon = 2 mL
3/4 teaspoon = 4 mL
1 teaspoon = 5 mL
1 tablespoon = 15 mL
2 tablespoons = 30 mL
1/4 cup = 60 mL
1/3 cup = 75 mL
1/2 cup = 125 mL
2/3 cup = 150 mL
3/4 cup = 175 mL
1 cup = 250 mL
2 cups = 1 pint = 500 mL
3 cups = 750 mL
4 cups = 1 quart = 1 L

VOLUME MEASUREMENTS (fluid)

1 fluid ounce (2 tablespoons) = 30 mL
4 fluid ounces (1/2 cup) = 125 mL
8 fluid ounces (1 cup) = 250 mL
12 fluid ounces (1 1/2 cups) = 375 mL
16 fluid ounces (2 cups) = 500 mL

WEIGHTS (mass)

1/2 ounce = 15 g
1 ounce = 30 g
3 ounces = 90 g
4 ounces = 120 g
8 ounces = 225 g
10 ounces = 285 g
12 ounces = 360 g
16 ounces = 1 pound = 450 g

DIMENSIONS

1/16 inch = 2 mm
1/8 inch = 3 mm
1/4 inch = 6 mm
1/2 inch = 1.5 cm
3/4 inch = 2 cm
1 inch = 2.5 cm

OVEN TEMPERATURES

250°F = 120°C
275°F = 140°C
300°F = 150°C
325°F = 160°C
350°F = 180°C
375°F = 190°C
400°F = 200°C
425°F = 220°C
450°F = 230°C

BAKING PAN SIZES

Utensil	Size in Inches/Quarts	Metric Volume	Size in Centimeters
Baking or Cake Pan (square or rectangular)	8×8×2	2 L	20×20×5
	9×9×2	2.5 L	23×23×5
	12×8×2	3 L	30×20×5
	13×9×2	3.5 L	33×23×5
Loaf Pan	8×4×3	1.5 L	20×10×7
	9×5×3	2 L	23×13×7
Round Layer Cake Pan	8×1½	1.2 L	20×4
	9×1½	1.5 L	23×4
Pie Plate	8×1¼	750 mL	20×3
	9×1¼	1 L	23×3
Baking Dish or Casserole	1 quart	1 L	—
	1½ quart	1.5 L	—
	2 quart	2 L	—